Dear Sarah,
I'm thrilled
to share
book with u
I'm sure our
we'll cross again
Best regards,
Patrick

THE
COLLABORATIVE
PATH

6 Steps for Better Communication, Problem-Solving, and Decision-Making

PATRICK AYLWARD

 FriesenPress

Suite 300 - 990 Fort St
Victoria, BC, V8V 3K2
Canada

www.friesenpress.com

Copyright © 2020 by Patrick Aylward
First Edition — 2020

bookqueries@collaborativepath.ca
www.collaborativepath.ca

ISBN
978-1-5255-5761-3 (Hardcover)
978-1-5255-5762-0 (Paperback)
978-1-5255-5763-7 (eBook)

1. BUS110000 BUSINESS & ECONOMICS / Conflict Resolution & Mediation

Distributed to the trade by The Ingram Book Company

Table of Contents

Dedication

I've rewritten this dedication more than I have any other piece of this book. Convention would suggest I should dedicate it to those who have been closest to me. Those closest to me know I didn't write this book for them and they already know I love them.

I want this dedication to go to those for whom this book is intended. So, who would that be? The group would include those who:

- want to experience less tension in their workplace and other relationships.
- want to escape the carnage of avoidance and people-pleasing in their personal lives, professional careers, partnerships, organizations and communities.

- sense that the conventional ways to communicate, problem-solve, and make decisions don't work, yet don't know what to do about it.

I dedicate this book to those who are frustrated with the status quo and offer them a better way forward, a collaborative path.

My Gratitude

It took a village to write this book!

Thank you to my early version readers, Garth and Lynn Turtle, Professor Carol Aylward, my son Sean Aylward, and Catherine Kennedy. What a horrible job that must have been, even though at the time I thought I was giving you a decent product. Sorry about that!

Thank you to my beta-readers, Jennifer MacLeod, Scott MacDonald, Nicole Priddle, Professor Carol Aylward, Mark Sutherland, Brenda Froese, Tara Kowalski, Professor Verner Smitheram, Jeff LeClair, and Sean Aylward for your honest input.

Thank you to Carol Aylward, Daryl Webber, Harold Dunstan, Karen MacDonald, and my children Sean, Vanessa, and Ryan, who pitched in with even more comments when I thought it was already perfect.

Thank you to the couple of hundred people who helped me to choose the title for this book. Wow, what a process that was! A special thank you to my daughter Samantha for coordinating that whole title-choosing exercise online.

Thank you to the inner circle – Carol, Daryl, Sean, and Verner – who read drafts multiple times, never got tired of helping me improve it, and made me take ownership for its originality when I tried to avoid doing so.

And, finally, thank you to Carol and Daryl, whose encouragement and contribution is impossible for me to describe in words, although I am making a feeble attempt.

Professor Carol Aylward inspired me with her own book and encouraged me to write this one. She advised me on the whole process and answered a ton of questions. She challenged me to the end (and beyond), edited everything I sent her, and was the first to tell me that my approach to this subject was ground-breaking. What a "coincidence" that she is in my life as I write this. Our running joke is that we are connected only because of her having had the patience to marry my oldest brother Gerard – twice! (Long story.)

Daryl Webber is a former federal government executive for whom I once worked. She is a spitfire with unlimited energy, intelligence, editorial and general wisdom, and an abundance of encouragement. When I told Daryl I was writing a book, without her knowing a single detail, she immediately raised her hand to offer to be my editor. Wow, what an amazing gift she has been in this process! What a "coincidence" that in my sixteen years as a federal public servant, my favorite boss and I continued to stay in touch for over ten years after we stopped working together, and she was there just when I needed her the most!

Carol and Daryl, my dynamic duo, you are not accidents in my life; the universe sent me you two to make sure I stayed on track. Without you, I would have gotten lost and stayed that way. Where Carol initiated the ownership conversation about the originality of my approach, Daryl pinned me down. It was a scary thing for me to accept that my approach is unique. Without you, *The Collaborative Path* would not exist.

Introduction

Trial lawyers might be the least collaborative members of the human race. I should know because that was my profession for sixteen years. When I was working as a lawyer, I assumed that how people communicated and problem-solved was fine 80 percent of the time. In the other 20 percent of cases, litigation was effective although expensive. It was the 80-20 rule: 80 percent of resources spent on 20 percent of the situations. The 80 seemed to be working together without any issues, and they didn't need to change. It was all about the 20, I thought.

I used to think that what I enjoyed about litigation was the thrill of winning. I now realize that my passion was about remedying injustice and unfairness.

After my work as a lawyer, I studied conflict resolution, and I thought I had found the Holy Grail to address the 20 percent far more cost-effectively and constructively through mediation than by litigation. It puzzled me that few others saw what I saw, however; private sector mediation was woefully slow, and I was starving. Money wasn't important to me. Eating was though, so I did the unthinkable for a dedicated entrepreneur: I became a public servant using my mediator skills for workplace conflict. In my new role, I loved how my work could change participants' attitudes and their workplace environments. I preached the positive side of conflict like it was the Gospel according to Saint Pat.

Then, it struck me! Having been exposed, first as a lawyer and then as a mediator, to the different ways that people work together – or don't – I realized the challenge was not how to address that problematic 20 percent, but the 80 percent. Within that group, communication and problem-solving is ineffective. We don't collaborate – even when we say we do.

Why don't we? Because no collaborative process model exists for the 80 percent, only for the 20 percent.

I suppose I always wanted to write a book, although I never thought I would. Now that it is almost complete, I'm struggling to explain here that this feels like I didn't have a choice but to write it. It sounds crazy and yet, the series of life and career events that led me here – things like being in two car accidents, either of which could have ended my life – makes me think that the universe kept me around for this reason. (On the other hand, perhaps it was the fleet of five argumentative kids in our house that drove me to write this book!)

Either way, the more I wrote, the more I became aware that my ideas are dramatically different from those of others in the fields of conflict resolution and mediation. As the contrast broadened page by page, my conviction grew that writing this book is exactly what I am supposed to be doing with my life.

A funny thing happens in mediation sometimes. At the end, participants wonder why they didn't resolve their situation sooner, and why they even needed a mediator at all. When people reviewed this book prior to its publication, they made similar comments:

"This is so simple!"

"Why doesn't everyone just use this collaborative model as the first option instead of conflict resolution as their last resort?"

"Why doesn't everyone see this?"

My hope is that when you read this book, it will change how you communicate, problem-solve, and make decisions in all aspects of your life. If you're not open to that, it's probably a good time, as they say in TV shows, for you to put this book down, back away slowly, and no one will get hurt.

If you *are* open to learning a simple six step collaborative process, let's get started.

CHAPTER ONE

What Happened to Getting to Yes?

What happened to the growth of "principled negotiations" that Roger Fisher and William Ury introduced in 1981 with *Getting to Yes?*[1] Millions read that book – in over thirty languages! Thousands of students and executives have been indoctrinated in that negotiation process in a wide variety of centres of learning. *Getting to Yes* has been described as "one of the best negotiation texts ever written."[2] Check where you want, *Getting to Yes* will be described as an incredibly influential book.

In *Getting to Yes*, Fisher and Ury laid out a universal negotiating process to replace an ineffectual negotiating model that they called "positional bargaining." Their "principled negotiation" process leads to better solutions while preserving or strengthening relationships among problem-solvers. As I point out later, collaboration is the deliberate pursuit of those dual outcomes: better solutions and stronger relationships. Therefore, principled negotiations is a truly collaborative approach. Because principled negotiations was designed to deliver those dual results, everyone was expected to embrace it as a superior process to positional bargaining.

Conflict, reduced to its two most basic components, is comprised of a problem plus tension. As an equation:

$$\text{Conflict} = \text{Problem} + \text{Tension}$$

The expectation was that their principled negotiation process, which I've described as collaborative in nature, could be used for

---

1   Roger Fisher and William Ury, *Getting to Yes: Negotiating Agreement Without Giving in* (New York: Penguin Books, 1981).

2   Keld Jensen, "Why Negotiators Still Aren't Getting to Yes," In *Forbes*, Feb. 05, 2013, accessed July 31, 2019, https://www.google.ca/amp/s/www.forbes.com/sites/keldjensen/2013/02/05/why-negotiators-still-arent-getting-to-yes/amp/.

any problem-solving to find a solution. Associating their collaborative process with resolving conflict should've opened up a world of opportunity for use of their collaborative approach in everyday communication, problem-solving, and analysis because conflict is everywhere. Had society embraced principled negotiations, we would communicate collaboratively, problem-solve collaboratively, and harness the diversity of thought that drives innovation. In short, we would be living in a culture of collaboration.

That better world should have evolved by now, yet we don't see a widespread use of principled negotiations and a culture of collaboration. Why not? If I could pick one word which stalled this shift toward collaboration in its tracks, that word is "conflict." The principled negotiation process presented in *Getting to Yes* became the foundation of *conflict resolution*. Conflict resolution is often described along the lines of assisting people to reach a solution that works for both parties, thereby generating a "positive result" from conflict. The implication that a positive side to conflict exists has been often repeated by conflict resolution professionals, psychologists, and academics.

As I will demonstrate in chapter five, there's no such thing as a positive side of conflict. That assertion is a grand illusion which is blocking both conflict resolution and collaboration.

Conflict is negative, as anyone embroiled in it knows. The stigma associated with conflict will continue to impede widespread use of conflict resolution. That is a serious issue because at the heart of conflict resolution is a "collaborative" problem-solving process. That process is "collaborative" because its use delivers dual outcomes: better solutions and stronger relationships. That collaborative process is incredibly under-utilized because people experience its effectiveness only when it is used to address conflict, and because of the stigma associated with conflict, that seldom happens. Widespread use of collaborative approaches thereby creating a culture of collaboration which should have followed the publication of *Getting to Yes* will happen only if we shift our focus from resolving conflict to strengthening collaboration.

Perhaps, if at least we made some effort to be collaborative when not in conflict, that would not be so bad. Some may think that they are being collaborative. In fact, lots of people often say they're being collaborative. Sadly, that is not true. Oblivious to the existence of a better way, society uses the "adjudicative" model for communication, problem-solving, and analysis. The adjudicative model has been the default since time immemorial.

The adjudicative model essentially involves identifying a couple of alternatives and debating the pros and cons of each in order to make a choice between them. That model may have been adequate when the world was less complex. However, going forward in the modern world, we need to move beyond problem-solving by identifying a couple of options and debating their pros and cons. We need a better alternative than the adjudicative model in every "workplace." By "workplace," I mean every team, group, community, organization, business, or government entity – anywhere people interact to get things done.

It has become the norm that a collaborative process is used only for conflict resolution, and the adjudicative model is used for everything else, in spite of the fact that a great deal of conflict is directly attributable to the use of the adjudicative model in the first place! Since most people avoid addressing conflict because of its complexity and stigma, very few are ever exposed to any collaborative process. Many concepts and terms within the sphere of conflict resolution reinforce that negativity, complexity, and avoidance. Consequently, the adjudicative model thrives while collaborative processes sit on the shelf. It is important to recognize that we're using an adjudicative model as the default, so that we can have a conversation about its value and limitations, and compare it with a superior alternative.

In order to create a culture of collaboration, we need to shift the focus from resolving conflict to strengthening collaboration. This shift will break our dependence on the adjudicative model. Whereas conflict and its resolution have a strong stigma, collaboration is positive and desirable. We need to stop waiting for conflict to brew to an almost irreparable level before we encourage people to be collaborative, akin to how the field of medicine has stopped waiting for people to have heart attacks before encouraging them to exercise and embrace a healthy diet. In the same way that the shift in medicine from illness to wellness is benefiting society, the shift from conflict to collaboration will have a similar positive impact. Embracing a collaborative model will equip society to face increasingly complex challenges, to leverage power in diverse talents and to empower the human spirit for innovation.

This book is about two things:

1. Why it's important that we stop focusing on conflict and shift to collaboration in order to break our dependence on the adjudicative model.
2. How we create a culture of collaboration by embedding a new model into everyday life.

CHAPTER TWO
The Origins of a Collaborative Approach

Around 1979, as a way to improve international negotiations, the Harvard Negotiation Project[3] conceived of a collaborative approach. As the project team watched the United States and Russia failing at negotiation, they examined the negotiation process. What they observed was that each nation would start from extreme positions and edge in small concessions toward some unknown middle point. Sometimes these nations found that point, and at other times, not so much.

To illustrate the model used in the arms race negotiations, it could be described this way:

> Russia: If you have 10 missiles, then we will build 20.
> USA: If you build 20, we will build 25.
> Russia: If you build 25, we will add 5 nuclear missiles.
> USA: Nuclear weapons threaten world peace; maybe we don't need 25.
> Russia: Maybe we would not build 5 nuclear missiles, if you would accept . . .

The project team called these back-and-forth exchanges "positional bargaining." Positional bargaining essentially employs the adjudicative model by using power and deceit as tools of persuasion. Each side presents its position as the only viable option, arguing that their position is unwavering and that the other's is untenable. They argue pros and cons in an effort to persuade the other, as they work slowly towards some compromise that neither like and both can live with.

---

3   *Harvard Negotiation Project* (1979), (published by The President and Fellows of Harvard College), accessed July 31, 2019, https://www.pon.harvard.edu/research_projects/harvard-negotiation-project/hnp/. This article is a good starting point to learn more about the project and its work.

If one were to have asked Russia what they wanted, the response might have been: recognition of communism as a legitimate form of government, influence on the world stage, and peace, security, and a good standard of living for their people. And what did the USA want? Basically the same things as Russia wanted, if you toss in democracy as a substitute for communism. The project team called the things that the nations wanted "interests."

The Harvard team wasn't seeing any of these interests being raised at the international negotiation table – just a contest over who had the bigger missile. (Looking back, that pattern has repeated itself through many eras and among many nations right up to present day.) The positions taken by the USA and Russia had very little chance of advancing their interests. The project team set out to develop a more effective way to reach agreements than through positional bargaining, one which would both give the participants the best chance to develop a good solution and at the same time improve their relationship – or at least, do it no harm. The project team developed an alternative process to positional bargaining, which they called "principled negotiations."

In 1981, Fisher and Ury published *Getting to Yes: Negotiating without Giving In*, in which they outlined a four-step process:

1. Separate the people from the problem.
2. Focus on interests not positions.
3. Generate a series of options before making any agreement.
4. Insist that the agreement be based on principles or objective criteria.

Fisher and Ury suggested that if nations talked about their interests, they would usually see that their interests were compatible (Fisher and Ury, 1981, 24), even if their positions were quite confrontational. They suggested that principled negotiations would not only improve solutions but also strengthen relationships (Fisher and Ury, 1981, 7).

As their analysis and research progressed, it became apparent that conflict existed at all levels and in all forums. It also became obvious that the same principles used to address conflict at international levels could be used with minimal modifications to address conflict at other levels of human interaction.

Not surprisingly, the principled negotiations approach became associated fairly early on with conflict resolution. Since 1981, the academic world continued to modify and improve that basic approach. In their second edition of *Getting to Yes*[4] (1991), Fisher and Ury noted that the field of negotiation and academic attention had exploded. Since 1981, except for *Beyond Reason*[5] and *The Power of a Positive No*[6], the Harvard group has published books that are mainly re-workings of familiar themes. *The Promise of Mediation,*[7] which challenged the focus on problem-solving in mediation, and proposed a model of empowerment and recognition would be another exception. Most of the literature in the conflict resolution domain seems to focus on the advantages of conflict resolution over formal processes, and how to benefit from conflict. Again, conflict is presented as having an upside.

Experts have debated, in chicken and egg fashion, whether the relationship between participants is transformed in the conflict resolution process so that they reach a solution, or whether they reach a solution that transforms the relationship. Academic works drew lines between such things as task conflict and personal conflict, healthy conflict and destructive conflict, and functional and dysfunctional conflict. They wrote about the idea that "conflict cannot be prevented."[8] If conflict cannot be prevented, then I suppose it makes sense to find a positive side to it. Similarly, it makes sense from that perspective to say that conflict shouldn't be feared, and indeed that there should be a sense of

---

4   Roger Fisher, William Ury and Bruce Patton, *Getting to Yes: Negotiating Agreement Without Giving In*, 2nd ed., (New York: Penguin Press, 1991).

5   Roger Fisher, *Beyond Reason: Using Emotions as You Negotiate* (New York: Penguin Books, 2006).

6   William Ury, *The Power of a Positive No: How to Say No and Still Get to Yes* (New York: Bantam Books, 2007).

7   Robert A. Baruch Bush and Joseph Folger, *The Promise of Mediation: Responding to Conflict through Empowerment and Recognition* (San Francisco: Jossey-Bass, 1994).

8   Jacob Bercovitch and Judith Fretter, *Regional Guide to International Conflict and Management from 1945 to 2003* (Washington, D.C.: CQ Press, 2004).

pride about being "conflict competent."[9] Consequently, today conflict resolution using some adaptation of principled negotiations is taught at a large number of universities and other centres of adult learning.

How does all this relate to collaboration? Looking at many definitions of collaboration, two essential components stand out: a sense of togetherness, and a sense of accomplishment. Put another way, it has a task and a relationship objective. As an equation:

Collaboration = Better Solutions + Stronger Relationships

"Collaboration" is the use of a problem-solving process to obtain the best solution in a way that improves relations among the problem-solvers. Being collaborative is advantageous for those who are task-oriented, because it serves their desire for optimal solutions. Equally, being collaborative is advantageous for those who are relationship-oriented, because it serves their desire for stronger relationships. Fisher and Ury's theory of principled negotiations[10] serves as the starting point for the development of a collaborative approach.

Describing collaboration as pursuing both better solutions and stronger relationships is also supported by the research of Kenneth Thomas and Ralph Kilmann. In 1974, they introduced their Thomas–Kilmann Conflict Instrument[11] (TKI). They identified five conflict response styles, depending on the balance between assertiveness and cooperativeness (very similar to task and relationship orientations). The TKI helps people to identify their dominant style based on their responses to a series of questions. The five styles identified by the TKI are:

---

9   Craig E. Rundle and Tim A. Flanagan, *Building Conflict Competent Teams* (San Francisco: Jossey-Bass, 2008).

10   One significant difference between the collaborative model being presented and the principled negotiations approach is that the latter was intended for use in negotiations, usually between two parties, and did not purport to have a use or application in the absence of an impasse. This collaborative model has broader application, even though as I point out later, it is not a "one size fits all'" solution.

11   Kenneth W. Thomas and Ralph H. Kilmann, *Thomas-Kilmann Conflict Mode Instrument*, (Tuxedo NY: Xicom, 1974), accessed July 31,2019, https://en.wikipedia.org/wiki/Thomas%E2%80%93Kilmann_Conflict_Mode_Instrument. This article has additional information on the development and history of the TKI.

- Compete
- Avoid
- Accommodate
- Compromise
- Collaborate

The diagram below shows these styles plotted against the task-relationship orientation axes.

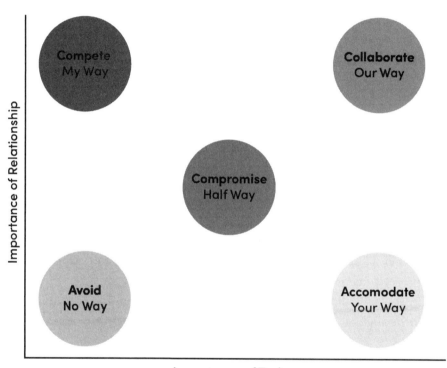

If these are conflict response styles, then by the definition of conflict above, these are also problem-solving styles. And, since communication is needed to solve problems, these are also communication styles.

In a problem-solving situation, a response is **competitive** if an individual promotes their solution, regardless of what impact it may have on relationships with others. A response is **avoidant** where an individual minimizes their input and their participation altogether. Similarly, when an individual's response is **accommodating** they give up on their idea about the best solution if they perceive that promoting it would negatively impact relationships. A **compromising** response would be to propose and invite trade-offs where each would be partially satisfied. Lastly, a response would be **collaborative** if the best possible solution were sought while at the same time having as positive an effect on relationships as possible. Obviously, in most situations being collaborative is a good thing because it is advantageous for both those who are task-oriented *and* those who are relationship-oriented.

While it's true that we each have a default response style, it's also true that we each use all five styles to some degree. In workshops, I've asked small groups to discuss what each person thought their default style was, and to get some feedback from others at their table. After that exercise, I asked them what the main theme of their discussion was. The almost universal response was that their style varied, depending on the situation. In other words, "it depends." The point of the exercise was to drive home the idea that we exercise choice about what style we use.

Therefore, being collaborative – or not – is a choice.

If being collaborative is a good thing generally, and people can choose to be collaborative, then strengthening the capacity for collaboration would be a good investment. And therefore, creating a culture of collaboration would be a great investment!

CHAPTER THREE

A New Collaborative Model – 6 Easy Steps

The opportunity to be collaborative is *not* restricted to conflict resolution. That opportunity arises with every problem we encounter and every interaction we have with others. I present below a new model of collaboration, which can be accomplished using six steps. This new model doesn't depend on conflict for its use or context.

The six steps are:

1. Set Parameters
2. Exchange Perspectives
3. Describe Issues
4. Identify Interests
5. Generate Options
6. Select Solutions

This model certainly has a basis in the mediation process used for conflict resolution, but its use is far more universal. In this collaborative model, each step has a single focus that makes it easy to learn and simple to apply. I describe them typically in the following manner:

The *Set Parameters* step is about creating a common understanding of how participants will engage in the problem-solving. The participants' conversation about *how* they will talk about *what* they need to talk about creates an atmosphere of safety and a shared understanding of the conversation's structure and their expectations.

The *Exchange Perspectives* step recognizes that what we may perceive to be the only solution or the truth about a situation is really only one person's perspective. Each person's perspective merits being heard. This step provides just that: the opportunity both to hear and to be heard. The power of listening is well understood both for problem solving and relationship-building. The listening that happens at this step serves to increase engagement and mutual understanding – even when the perspectives are vastly different.

The ***Describe Issues*** step accomplishes what Fisher and Ury called "separating the people from the problem" (Fisher and Ury, 1981, 30). To do that, the issue(s) arising from the perspectives exchanged in step two is expressed in such a way that it:

- doesn't suggest a solution
- doesn't identify a dichotomy for choice
- doesn't attach fault or blame to either participant for the problem itself

The use of non-judgmental language separates the people from the problem because it ensures that neither participant senses blame for the problem as it exists. When the issue is described neutrally, each participant can see that they have room to talk about the things that are important to them; that they are not being judged; and, that the issue is not slanted to favour any particular outcome.

The ***Identify Interests*** step is about exploring perspectives more deeply. Each participant knows how they think the problem should be resolved. Fisher and Ury would say these instinctive first solutions are "positions." This step is about determining what informs those positions. Fisher and Ury would say these informing factors are "interests." As the field of interest-based approaches developed, interests are now often said to include:

- needs
- wants
- hopes
- fears
- concerns
- assumptions
- values
- beliefs

Put in a very simple way, interests are the broader things people want (or want to avoid), which in turn makes them think that their position would be a good solution. The greater the level of tension, the more obscured these interests become as people become increasingly entrenched in their positions. When they are so focused on their positions, they can neither see their own interests nor those of others.

The importance of focusing on interests instead of positions is two-fold:

1. Whereas positions lend themselves to only one way of being satisfied, interests can be met by a far broader range of options.
2. Even when people have a big gap between their positions, they often have very compatible interests.

The *Identify Interests* step brings those interests to light. As that illumination of compatible interests happens, participants gain a sense of appreciation of the other person, increasing mutual understanding. The interests identified serve another purpose: those once hidden interests that drove their initial perspectives, positions and solutions will now serve as the springboard for expanding options.

Generate Options is where the participants create new ideas to address their situation. They do this by asking themselves "what could we do to resolve the issues we are working on in ways that would satisfy the interests we just noted?" The key to brainstorming is to avoid early evaluation of options because early evaluation kills creativity. No evaluation is needed at this point anyway because evaluation will occur later. At the end of *Generate Options*, the participants who had started with two positions (two options) now have a broad array from which to choose.

Finally, we are ready to *Select Solutions*. Again, this step continues to demonstrate the logic inherent in this collaborative model, because the selection is essentially accomplished by the participants asking themselves, "which of the options generated best address the issues in a way that satisfies our interests?" When the best solution components are selected, they are reality-tested to ensure that they are feasible to implement. In this way, the responsibilities around implementation for each participant become clear.

This new collaborative model has logic and simplicity that can be applied to any problem and incorporated into any decision-making or analytical process. It can be used as a guide for any conversation. It is a matter of choosing to use it.

CHAPTER FOUR

The Adjudicative Model – Communication, Analysis, and Decision-Making

We don't use a collaborative model to communicate. Nor to solve problems. Nor for analysis to make decisions. We continue to stick with the adjudicative model as our default, one which has been popular since the era of ancient Greece, with Socrates, Plato, Aristotle, and elevated by the skills in rhetoric and oratory during the era of the Roman Empire with men like Cicero. Frequently, this model is called "rights-based" or "distributive" in contrast to "interest-based" and "integrative." Personally, I dislike all of those labels because I don't think they mean much to the guy on the street. Most people have a sense of what collaborative means; similarly, they understand that an adjudicative model is about debating the pros and cons of the choices available.

This next section is a more expansive explanation of the adjudicative model and shows how people typically use it. The adjudicative model has four steps:

1. Statement of Issues
2. Identification of Options
3. Analysis
4. Selection/Recommendation of Preferred Solution

In *Statement of Issues*, the issue is often tilted toward one of the options that will be presented. At best, the issue is framed as a fair choice among two or three options. Even when the issue is framed more openly as a "whether, and if so, how-to-do-something" sort of question, that phraseology is usually intended only for the appearance of objectivity. The decision has been taken and the analysis is intended to support the ratification of that decision.

Identification of Options typically is as simple as identifying two or three already-known options. No effort is made to invent any new ones. Usually, these "options" are the participants' positions or bottom lines. Often, the approach is to narrow the options to a dichotomy where one solution is desirable, and the other is far less so.

Analysis is an examination of the context within which the decision is taken and that may include risk management analysis or other factors at play. That said, the pros and cons associated with each option are the main focus of the discussion. The objective of the analysis is to demonstrate persuasively why one option is better than the other(s).

Selection/Recommendation involves summarizing the persuasive argument in favour of the preferred solution, usually to support a decision already made.

The Adjudicative Model – Communication

The adjudicative model is commonly used in everyday communication – not all the time of course, yet often enough to make relationships difficult. Obviously, today's communication model isn't working! When is communication *not* the number one or two issue in any workplace experiencing challenges?

If you want to do a quick check on what model is being used for communication in your workplace, listen for two things:

1. How often is the word "but" being used?
2. How many of the questions being posed are closed versus open?

Put simply, closed questions seek to verify specific information; open questions seek to explore background and context, thereby gaining additional information.

If you are hearing argumentative statements, no matter how softly they are being asserted, and if you are hearing the words "but" or "however" within the first five words of a response, then you are almost certainly observing debate and persuasion at work. If you are hearing mostly closed questions, then you are listening to people who have made their mind up about the "right" outcome, people who are communicating without any spirit of curiosity. If you are still not certain, check out the listening styles of the participants. Do they seem to be listening to deepen their understanding of the other's perspective, or are they just waiting for an opening to respond, rather than even listening at all? If you are seeing people listening to respond, then you are watching a debate – the adjudicative model – as the basis for communication.

The Big Three Conversations – the Bottle, the Blurt, and the Blab

In most workplaces, three conversations happen almost every day, and these conversations have a significantly negative impact. The Big Three are the *Bottle*, the *Blurt*, and the *Blab*.

The *Bottle* is the conversation where Paul is upset with Kate about something that she did or didn't do, something that he doesn't like, or something that is not working for him at all. For any number of reasons, Paul chooses to avoid talking with Kate about it. He makes excuses for her: "maybe Kate was just having a bad day – I will let it go this time." He makes excuses for himself: "maybe if I had approached things differently, she would not have done that, so next time I will just deal with it by handling my part differently." He justifies his choice: "I suppose Kate is just like that, probably nothing is going to change her;" or, "I could make matters worse . . . I better just leave it alone." Perhaps Paul uses all three of those avoidance thoughts and more – no matter. The end result is that the only conversation he is having with Kate is the one bottled up inside his head. This conversation could go on for months. Kate, on the other hand, is carrying on, thinking that things are going well and that she and Paul have a good working relationship.

Wait, though. The pressure is building inside that bottle. Here comes the *Blurt*. After some period of bottling things up, Paul is pretty tense. Kate does something again that irritates him – perhaps she puts the staple through the wrong side of a presentation, or one page is upside down, or she puts something in the wrong place. In any event, put in perspective, Kate's act or omission is pretty tame. Paul's reaction is immediate and harsh. He blurts out something mean-spirited, condescending, or sarcastic. Kate is shocked. She has no idea where this outburst is coming from. Perhaps Paul throws in a couple of other irritants from the past, which Kate is hearing for the first time. She wonders what is wrong with Paul. She is bewildered and offended. She attacks, is righteously indignant, or walks away in disgust. Blurt conversations don't end well.

Now, Paul might not *Blurt*. He has another option: he can *Blab* with his colleague, Mary. This conversation can take a few forms. One might be Paul saying something like, "I like Kate, but have you ever noticed that she . . . " It could be quite a passive comment like, "I don't know how I am ever going to survive working with Kate." Or, it could be said with higher energy: "Oh my gawd, Mary! You would not believe what Kate just did – again!"

In any of those three blabs, Paul influences Mary's perception of Kate. He conveys two incredibly damaging, non-verbal messages to Mary about Kate:

1. If Kate is like this with me, you should watch out because she will be like that with you.
2. If I am upset with Kate, you should be too.

The *Blab* is a classic conversation using the adjudicative model: the Blabber is right and what the other person did is wrong. The *Blab* is the most insidious of the Big Three. In the *Bottle*, Paul harms himself; in the *Blurt*, he harms himself and Kate; in the *Blab*, he harms the whole workplace.

How much talent do workplaces lose as a result of the Big Three? How many people change jobs, leave teams, or quit volunteering because of these conversations? Even when this talent remains in the workplace, how much time is lost and energy expended unproductively because of these conversations?

What would you guess would be the average amount of time used unproductively per week relating to conflict at work? Let me recap the evidence of three studies, which reached pretty much the same conclusion about the range of time wasted. *Uncovering the Hidden Costs of Interpersonal Conflicts: A Study of Selected Hotels in Kenya* (2016) states: "When compared with the results of similar surveys referred to in the theoretic part of this thesis, the total of 3.2 hours per week per person spent in dealing with badly managed conflict fall within the range assessed elsewhere."[12] *Controlling Conflict Costs: The Business Case of Conflict Management* (2011) states: "The survey conducted by the author in UNHCR [United Nations High Commissioner for Refugees] found that employees spend 2.7 hours a week in badly managed conflict."[13] *Workplace Conflict and How Businesses Can Harness It To Thrive* (2008) indicates: ". . . we found that U.S. employees spend 2.8 hours per week dealing with conflict."[14] (Note that this study found 2.1 hours on average across the nine nations that they explored.)

Unless your workplace is vastly different than those studied and somehow miraculously falls outside that range, you can do the math using 2.5 hours as a minimum, multiplied by the average hourly salary, multiplied by the number of employees in the workplace, multiplied by 50 weeks. This will calculate the annual cost of conflict in your workplace.

A significant portion of that loss would be avoided if those engaging in the Big Three used a collaborative model to communicate. The impacts on both solutions and relationships would be significantly more positive, and time would be used more efficiently. When I was working with a government department in 2011, I developed a one-day workshop on collaborative communication and delivered it to

---

12   Mukolwe, Eunice and Eliza Buyeke Ogucha, "Uncovering the Hidden Costs of Interpersonal Conflicts: A Study of Selected Hotels in Kenya," Journal of Tourism, Hospitality and Sports, vol.17 (2016), accessed July 31, 2019, https://iiste.org/Journals/index.php/JTHS/article/download/29143/29932.

13   Helmut Buss, "Controlling Conflict Costs: The Business Case of Conflict Management," *Journal of the International Ombudsman Association*, vol.4, number 1 (2011), accessed July 31, 2019, http://fpombudsman.org.s195742.gridserver.com/wp-content/uploads/2014/11/Helmut-Buss_Controlling-Conflict-Costs-The-Business-Case-of-Conflict-Management-2011.pdf.

14   "Workplace Conflict and How Businesses Can Harness It To Thrive," CPP Global Human Capital Report, (July, 2008), accessed July 31, 2019, http://img.en25.com/Web/CPP/Conflict_report.pdf.

some 2,000 employees. Thirty days after each workshop, participants were asked about their use of the collaborative communication skills from the training and its impact on their workplace. Their choices about the extent of use ranged from no use to using everything. In relation to the impact of using the skills, their response choices ranged from making things worse to increasing efficiency and strengthening problem-solving. The results indicated that more than 80 percent of participants used the collaborative communication skills with a significantly positive impact.

In Chapter 14, I explain how the Big Three destructive conversations can be replaced with everyday collaborative conversations using three skills that mirror and incorporate the new collaborative model:

1. C-Message
2. De-escalation and Re-orientation
3. Sounding Board

Email isn't the problem – the adjudicative message is the problem!

Increasingly in society today, electronic communication is the norm. Even meetings are frequently held "electronically." The advantage of electronic communication is obviously efficiency. Perhaps there is also an advantage in "thinking time," allowing participants more time to engage the brain ahead of the mouth – or in this case, fingers. In answer to the Dr. Phil question "how is that working for you?" many would respond that it's not working so well.

You may be familiar with the studies analyzing messages we convey using body language, tone, or words. Dr. Albert Mehrabian, author of *Silent Messages*,[15] conducted several studies on nonverbal communication. He found that seven-percent of any message about feelings and attitudes is conveyed through words, 38 percent through certain vocal elements, and 55 percent through nonverbal elements. Of course, in electronic communication, vocal elements and

---

15   Albert Mehrabian, *Silent Messages: Implicit Communication of Emotions and Attitudes* (Belmont, CA: Wadsworth, 1972).

non-verbal elements are non-existent. Their absence doesn't mean though that only seven-percent of the message is conveyed. In their absence, we extract 100 percent of the message from what we have to work with – the electronic communication, the relational context, and our experiences.

This research suggests that greater care is needed to increase the likelihood that the message is received as intended. Modern add-ons like emojis – from smiley faces to angry ones – are frequently used to supplement the context and intent. My inclination is to not blame the electronics for the miscommunications and negative impacts on relationships. If the technology is being used to communicate ideas using an adjudicative model, then regardless of how many emojis one adds, the result and impact is the same. The message received is: "These are the two choices. I like option A because of these reasons. My ideas are better than yours." *THAT* message lands the same, whether face to face, by telephone, video conference, text or email.

The Adjudicative Model – Analysis

The adjudicative model generates analysis to support "decision-making," which is fundamental to society. In a knowledge-based economy, analytical skills are highly valued. For governments, solid policy and program decisions rely heavily on analysis. The same is true for non-governmental organizations and for private sector enterprises. Without analysis, innovation and execution would depend on . . . well, luck, I suppose.

Just how solid is this typical "decision-making" analysis? I place "decision-making" in quotation marks because under the adjudicative model, it is not decision-making analysis taking place at all. Instead, it is "decision-taken" analysis (i.e., to support the decision already taken). In government, Memoranda to Cabinet, Issue Papers, and Briefing Notes are typically prepared using that model. That adjudicative model is prevalent not only in government, but also in many areas of the private sector, where business plans and action strategies are developed using it, too. It is not necessarily a flawed method *if* the decision taken is the optimal one, and only after a full range of options has been considered. In turn, a range of options cannot be said to be full unless at least one option has been developed to meet every key interest identified. Key interests, though, are not identified at any step in the adjudicative model. Some would argue that the identification of key interests and the generation of options to meet those interests probably occurred before the decision was taken. If that is so, then all may be well and good. In my experience, however, organizations do not regularly use any interest identification process that is similar to the collaborative model described earlier.

The adjudicative model presents persuasive arguments to justify a decision already taken. When the supposed analysis starts, the options are presented as equally viable. The existence of a preferred option, from the outset, is not made known. Instead, the persuasive arguments are presented as if solid analysis led to the best of the options available – which happens to be the preferred option all along. The actual decision-making does not, in fact, use a process designed to reach the optimal decision. The presumption is made that the preferred option is the optimal decision.

There is nothing wrong with persuasiveness. There *is* something wrong with accepting persuasive argument as analysis. There is a *lot* wrong with disguising decision-taken analysis as decision-making analysis. Even looking within only the federal government system in Canada in the last twenty years, some pretty major initiatives have failed miserably because key interests like capacity, cost effectiveness, and efficiency, were not addressed. While you may not be able to access the analysis done to enable the government of the day to authorize those initiatives, you can bet your last dollar that the analysis was done using the adjudicative model to support the ratification of decisions that were already taken. Using this new collaborative model, such key interests would have been identified before options were developed. The options would be assessed based on the extent to which they addressed the key interests, and the selected option would be reality-tested before being implemented.

These two models are dramatically different. The adjudicative model starts at the desired solution and works back to why it is the right decision relative to its advantages against different options. In comparison, the collaborative model starts at the problem and works forward towards the optimal solution, whatever it might be, by identifying the key interests that need to be addressed and only then developing options that could serve those interests. The adjudicative model is oriented to a solution known at the outset, whereas the collaborative model is exploratory. The quality of the analysis in the adjudicative model is assessed on the basis of how well the rationale supports the decision taken. Oddly enough, that analysis is not judged on the quality of the decision taken, or upon whether the decision taken was strategic or innovative. In my experience, participants evaluate the effectiveness of the collaborative model based upon the quality of the solutions that it generates and the extent to which those solutions satisfy the interests identified.

The adjudicative model supports the decision taken. The collaborative model supports decision-making.

Now, that said, you may have noticed that I've just used the adjudicative analysis model to present the argument that a collaborative model is superior to the adjudicative model. I framed the dichotomy between "decision-making" and "decision-taken" analysis – slanting the issue by my word choices to the conclusion I want you to accept. My "analysis" didn't talk about any key interests that would be addressed with an optimal analytical model, nor did I present a "door #3." I presented only two choices. Without even thinking about it, I defaulted to the adjudicative model. This demonstrates how deeply the use of the adjudicative model is embedded within our society. Even those trained in the principled negotiations approach default to the adjudicative model as second nature! And, if we continue to use collaborative processes only to address conflict, a collaborative model will *never* become mainstream. If this collaborative model is in fact a superior one for communication, problem-solving, and analysis, then we as individuals, as organizations, and as a society, are losing out because collaborative approaches have been restricted to only the realm of conflict resolution. This restriction is a direct result of associating principled negotiations with conflict. Conflict is negative and people avoid addressing conflict because of that stigma. Fisher and Ury could never have expected that conflict would serve as a constraint on the use of their process: they stated "conflict is a growth industry" (Fisher and Ury, 1981, 6).

The Adjudicative Model – Decision-Making by Debate and Vote

Most democratic institutions are pre-disposed to rely upon the adjudicative model for true decision-making, not just for analysis to support the decision taken as described above. The most common form of governance in democracies is by motions that are debated, and then voted upon. The debate is one of western society's most ancient models of decision-making. The process is so engrained that debating societies and clubs exist as a means of honing and demonstrating the skills and abilities associated with the process.

Companies – and most if not all unincorporated groups in western society – express their actions and decisions as approved motions that are presented, debated and voted upon with some level of adherence to *Robert's Rules of Order*.[16] While there's a legal requirement that companies express their actions in motions and resolutions recorded in minutes, the decision-making doesn't need to be conducted using an adjudicative model. The actual decision-making can be by consensus and then recorded as a minute to reflect the passing of a motion.

What happens in groups that make decisions using the adjudicative model by debating and voting? Very early on, the issue becomes framed as a choice between limited options. In a small number of situations, the options are refined or expanded upon as the debate progresses. In my experience, the frequency and degree to which the quality of options is improved, compared with the quantity of decisions made in this fashion, is minimal.

---

16   *Robert's Rules of Order* is the book on parliamentary procedure for parliamentarians and anyone involved in an organization, association, club, or group and the authoritative guide to smooth, orderly, and fairly-conducted meetings and assemblies.

Typically, only a couple of voices are heard, not the perspective of each participant in the group. The remaining members speak for or against the motion only in their votes. As the group weighs pros and cons of the options, the most common experience is that factions become increasingly polarized. Sarcasm and ridicule are not unheard of as debating tools. Quick-witted comments intended to show the weakness of an opposing viewpoint and calls for a quick or early vote shutting down debate will increase the sense of polarization.

In a debate, each idea and thought presented is fair game for evaluation and judgment. This evaluation starts when the first idea or motion is presented, and it continues throughout the debate. As the debate winds down, a final decision is recorded. Sometimes, the one with the loudest voice prevails. At other times, people give up when they sense they aren't being heard. Still other times, the debate is won by the person with the best oratory skills, not necessarily the best solution.

The debate may happen in an orderly and respectful fashion that showcases *Robert's Rules of Order*. Despite that, the final outcome is unlikely to be as optimal a solution as a collaborative model would have delivered. Just as significantly, although the cracks may be slow to appear, the impact on present and future relationships among the decision makers is not as positive as it would be if the group had used a collaborative model of decision-making. Given time, the cracks will surface and grow.

The debating process takes its toll on talent. Many a valuable board member or group participant has walked away from a worthy cause because of divisiveness, dominance by a few, being unheard, and feeling marginalized. It was not that those departing didn't have something valuable to contribute.

Another consequence of the debate and vote process is a tendency for participants on the "losing" side to "agree and undermine." Going in, participants know that they are using a "majority rules" approach. The corollary of the open debate is acceptance of the outcome, win or lose. Accordingly, one would expect that the losing side would be prepared to accept and implement the decision of their committee.

That is often not what happens. Instead, the losing side accepts the decision on the surface and then works feverishly to undermine its implementation.

In stark contrast, participants in decision-making using the new collaborative model are highly likely to support the ultimate solution, even if it isn't perfect. They will have been heard, they will have influenced ideas, and they will have had their interests reflected in options generated. Patrick Lencioni makes the point that when the debate is full and people do not fear conflict, then participants will typically "disagree and commit"[17] in a worst-case scenario. A simple example of this approach is seen on televised matches in the sport of curling when four players on the team discuss a shot, generate several options, and arrive at the final decision. Then, even if some of them don't see the shot chosen as the best option, all four players talk about what they need to do in order to execute it as well as possible.

A collaborative decision-making model encourages full group participation. Collaboration treats each perspective as having value and as unique. The objective of this collaborative model is to harness the wealth in the diversity of perspectives. Whereas the adjudicative model uses evaluation of ideas to support persuasion, the new collaborative model encourages creative solutions. In this collaborative model, evaluation doesn't happen until very late in the decision-making process.

No Time to Be Collaborative?

The extra time it takes for collaboration is the most common concern I've heard voiced. It's true that in the typical problem-solving conversations happening in a workplace, being collaborative and using collaborative tools usually does take more time than it does to make a choice between two options using the adjudicative model. It may take twenty minutes instead of ten in many cases. Some, explaining that they do not have time to have collaborative conversations, say they prefer to be very assertive and direct. They say they do not have that extra ten minutes. Really? Remember those studies on time wasted

---

17   Patrick Lencioni, *The Five Dysfunctions of a Team* (San Francisco: Jossey-Bass, 2002) 95-96.

unproductively because of conflict – about 2.5 hours per person per week?

An additional concern expressed about collaborative processes is that they can be too inclusive and represent too many perspectives. The common expression that comes to mind is "too many cooks spoil the broth." Related to that concern is that as more key interests are identified, the solution will become too complex. Interest identification, though, is at the heart of the collaborative model; interests are identified through the exploration of perspectives. The greater the number and diversity of problem-solving perspectives, the greater the array of interests identified. Consequently, solutions tend to be more complex and inclusive, which in turn increases the time taken in collaboration. This is an incrementally minimal time investment compared to *not* being collaborative!

The other side of the coin is that in any group, all of those "too many" viewpoints already exist, so to continue the first analogy the "too many cooks" are in the kitchen anyway. The difference in using a collaborative model instead of the adjudicative one is that their viewpoints are leveraged, and everyone contributes to the work rather than resisting and undermining the outcome as in an adjudicative model. This happens all the time in change initiatives. Frequently, the resistance is "managed" by isolating those resisting. This strategy typically has two consequences: the talent of the resisters is largely wasted on "busy" work, and the majority group later encounters – much to their surprise – some of the pitfalls about which the resisters were trying to warn them.

Additionally, as referenced earlier, studies show a big loss of productive time wasted on conflict in the workplace within an adjudicative model atmosphere. Employing this collaborative communication model, people can have productive conversations efficiently, and at the same time both strengthen relationships and get more done (better solutions.) Therefore, there is a double recovery on the time invested: recovery of some of the time that would otherwise be wasted on conflict; a second recovery from the better solution and reduced resistance during its implementation.

Lastly, note that this new collaborative model takes far less time to use than is perceived at the outset. Like any process, once participants become accustomed to its use, the flow is more efficient. So, are you really thinking that you don't have time to be collaborative? I suggest that you don't have the time *NOT* to be collaborative.

Some readers – especially those in government and other bureaucratic organizations – will think that it's more important to be "integrated" and "strategic" than collaborative in their activities. Being integrated might be thought of as having to do with creating synergies and horizontal alignment of initiatives and resources. Being strategic is about aligning vertically with mandate, mission, and vision, and ensuring the decisions are appropriately forward-looking.

It's far easier to be integrated in planning and strategic in decision-making using a collaborative rather than the adjudicative model. For example, let's take any enterprise with a financial unit, a sales unit, and a marketing unit. Each unit needs money and people in order to get work done. These resources are finite, and resources spent in one place means there's less to spend in others. Yet, the success of the enterprise depends on all units being successful, doing good work, and working together. In an adjudicative model, the units compete for resources. In the adjudicative debate, each unit will likely suggest that investing in them is the best use of resources for the enterprise. The approach remains a zero-sum game: one for me equals one less for you, net sum equals zero. Zero-sum approaches do not lend themselves to either integration or strategic decision-making. They create the same relationship impacts as debate and vote governance does.

How often do people say things like "around here, the sales department calls all the shots" or "they talk about customer service, but it's really whatever the bean counters say. They have all the power"? This is the classic impact of adjudicative decision-making: one unit perceives itself as the powerless "poor cousin." That approach doesn't improve productivity or morale. It definitely doesn't advance integrated or strategic decision-making. Continuing to use the adjudicative model as your default will rob your business or organization of opportunities.

CHAPTER FIVE

The Grand Illusion: The "Positive Side" of Conflict

In the introduction, I challenged the idea that there is a positive side to conflict. That longstanding "sales pitch" is all but proclaimed as universal truth. It appears in many descriptors of conflict:

Conflict can be constructive.

How conflict is dealt with determines whether it is positive or negative.

There is an opportunity to benefit from conflict.

Its publication as truth also has taken many forms – posters, articles, books, and workshops. Craig Rundle has suggested the development of "conflict competence"[18] as an organizational goal, and certainly as a skill for leaders.

If conflict being positive were equivalent to the idea that diversity of perspectives fuels creativity, that proposition would sound correct. In fact, Doug Hall in *Jump Start Your Business Brain*[19] provided evidence that demonstrates this theory, the direct proportionality between diversity and creativity, to be valid. The importance of diversity to creativity, though, is not at all the point intended by the idea of a "positive side" to conflict.

Let's examine this proposition for a moment: what's so positive about conflict? The experience of being in a conflict is not a positive one, not for the participants, and certainly not in the moment. What is supposed to be positive is that, *if properly addressed*, the situation gives rise to a positive outcome, some new solution, idea or result. From that positive outcome, it is argued that because the outcome

---

18   Craig E. Rundle, *Becoming a Conflict Competent Leader: How You and Your Organization Can Manage Conflict Effectively* (San Francisco: Jossey-Bass, 2013).

19   Doug Hall, *Jump Start Your Business Brain: Win More, Lose Less and Make More Money* (Cincinnati: Brain Brew Books, 2002) 235-265.

was typically a better one that either participant had envisaged at the outset, then the conflict was worthwhile. It's an "all's well that ends well" argument.

The idea presupposes that if it were not for the conflict, the participants could never, or would never, have arrived at the better place, solution, or result. Hmmm, is that true? If so, then what did they do differently to get there? The answer is that they engaged in a collaborative process, isn't it? If so, then the proposition must be that people can engage in collaborative processes that produce positive outcomes only if and when there is conflict. Conflict leads – or forces – them to be collaborative. Really?

A dispute, impasse, or conflict is *not* a prerequisite for using a collaborative process. Think about this: if we can use a collaborative process *after* the point when the situation could be described as a conflict, what prevents us from using that collaborative process *before* that point? The real truth is that the association of the use of collaborative approaches with conflict is no longer valuable – if it ever was. Note that *Getting to Yes* was published back in 1981 – almost 40 years ago. Four decades later, how often do you see the basic principled negotiations process being used? Almost never! What happened?

In the immediate aftermath of *Getting to Yes*, interest was intense and grew rapidly. When the second edition of *Getting to Yes* was published in 1991, the authors wrote in the preface:

> *In the last ten years negotiation as a field for academic and professional concern has grown dramatically. New theoretical works have been published, case studies have been produced, and empirical research undertaken. Ten years ago almost no professional school offered courses on negotiation; now they are all but universal.*

Let's ask a classic mediation question about this sales pitch that is so universal in conflict resolution: *"What is it about conflict being positive that is important to you?"* The answers that practitioners might provide would include items like:

- History
- Culture
- Being valued (as a professional)
- Having a context (for the mediation work)
- Creating opportunities
- Defining a sphere of influence/expertise
- Being different

All those responses make sense. The practice of conflict resolution grew out of an analysis of international conflict. The association with conflict is woven into the fabric of the culture of the practice, so much so that it is part of the label "Conflict Resolution." Those who are experts in adjudicative responses to disputes have a sense of being valued for the skills they bring to the adjudicative arena. Naturally, practitioners want to experience a similar sense of being valued for what they bring to society. In almost every mediation process, at least one participant going in is very skeptical that anything positive will result. When the positive outcome is achieved, participants often leave with a sense of wonderment about the power of mediation. Being able to produce positive results from an agonizing conflict sounds like an amazing value added by this expertise.

To a certain extent, conflict for specialists in the field is like electricity to electricians, building plans to carpenters, and cars to mechanics. It sets the context for when people should call in an expert. Similarly, being associated with conflict creates a list of opportunities to showcase the skills and grow demand. Litigation lawyers deal with injuries, contracts, and insurance claims in court. Labour lawyers deal with grievances, collective agreements, and labour codes before boards and arbitrators. Mediators deal with people in conflict. Conflict defines the sphere of expertise.

Doug Hall says that to sell an idea, it's critical to demonstrate a "dramatic difference" (ibid., 131-136) from other ideas. To be not only comfortable with conflict, but also able to find a positive side to conflict, that is a dramatically different contribution than that provided by adjudicative-support experts such as lawyers, accountants, and expert witnesses. Looking at it in this way, lots of good-sounding reasons exist for the pitch that conflict is positive.

Many, including me, have tried to make that pitch, and anecdotally, it seems that their experience has been the same as mine. Most people intellectually grasp the concept of a positive side of conflict; some will buy it fully and repeat the pitch to others. Yet, they know that if it's their *own* situation, then the lost energy and unproductive time flowing from their conflict is *not* positive. The strain placed on their relationships during the period of conflict and any scars and negative memories that may endure, those impacts are *not* positive. The ordinary person's experience of conflict is typically negative.

The sales pitch that conflict is positive should be embroidered and framed: "There is a big difference between good-sounding reasons, and good sound reasoning."

History is important and at the same time, this expression is also true: "The problem with the past is that there is no future in it." Culture gives a sense of belonging, which is important. Culture also contributes to stagnation and its protective approach to the status quo makes culture a huge obstacle to change. Similarly, a fine line exists between being valued for a skill set applicable to a situation and being valued only when that situation arises. Sometimes, when we see a source of opportunity, we look only at that one source – a tunnel vision effect – and miss out on everything else.

The "positive side of conflict" sales pitch has created tunnel vision. It was thought that associating principled negotiations with conflict and portraying conflict as positive would open up a world of opportunity. Despite refinements, the principled negotiations model is ignored and seldom used. As long as it is associated with conflict, that will *never* change. Conflict is **_not_** a growth industry. The idea that there is a positive side to conflict is, sadly, a grand illusion – one that in the past I also bought into.

CHAPTER SIX

Reinforcing the Stigma and Complexity of Conflict

If the earlier portions of this book suggest that conflict resolution is a bad thing, or that conflict competence is a useless skill set, then I have not been clear. Conflict resolution is incredibly powerful and effective. Similarly, conflict competence, the ability to communicate and work through situations of conflict and even to prevent conflict from escalating, is very useful in situations of conflict. The problem that arises is that if only a small number of people use conflict resolution approaches or work to develop that competence, or if they use that competence only when conflict has been well-escalated, then it really doesn't matter how valuable either are: *no critical mass will ever exist to support widespread use of any collaborative process.* Perhaps that's the greatest flaw in setting "conflict competence" as an organizational objective.

Conflict Competence

When I raised with colleagues this idea that we no longer need our skills, processes, techniques, and methodologies to be associated with conflict, and that instead we need to create a culture of collaboration in order to advance society, many balked. Instead, they insisted that we need to have a vision based on conflict competence as the workplace ideal.

Even if everyone in conflict were to use conflict resolution instead of avoidance as their key strategy when conflict arises, and even if everyone were equipped with some "conflict competency" skill set, though, that still would mean that they would use those skills only after conflict had developed, and only from that point until it had been resolved. What would they do the rest of the time? They would continue to use the adjudicative model – the model, as indicated above, that automatically triggers a great deal of conflict in the first place. To continue my earlier analogy about the shift in the emphasis in medicine from illness to wellness, this is like a doctor who treats their stroke or heart attack patient with a wellness approach of healthy diet and exercise, and then tells the patient to stick with that until the critical period has passed. When the critical period has passed, the patient resumes their old lifestyle until another stroke or heart attack occurs, caused by the same lifestyle that caused the first episode.

Taking a moment to reach out to those who advocate for conflict competence as an organizational goal, I see conflict competence in a different light, or from a different perspective, than most. When I read Kramer's writing about conflict competence, I notice he talks about five major trends that he thinks will make problem-solving more complex going forward[20]:

- The emergence of new political and social agendas in the workplace
- The increasing diversity of the workforce
- The growing role of information technology
- The move away from traditional hierarchical bureaucracies, and
- The globalization of the world economy and markets

While Kramer uses the words "conflict competence," he does so to describe a yet-to-be-defined set of skills to address tensions that will arise because of those trends, both at an individual and organizational level. When you think about skills and processes to harness diversity by building solutions that incorporate elements of widely-different perspectives, how different does that sound from the culture of collaboration I'm writing about? If Kramer had described it as collaboration competence, perhaps this book wouldn't even be necessary. Note that he doesn't say what will comprise "conflict competence," or what skills or processes will be required to maintain "organizational effectiveness" (ibid.) in the face of those five trends.

---

20   Roderick M. Kramer, *Negotiation as a Social Process* (Thousand Oaks, CA: Sage Publications, 1995) 191.

Craig Rundle has latched on to the idea of "conflict competence" as a skill set for resolving conflicts when they arise by leveraging the "positive" side of conflict, which, as explained above, is a grand illusion. His approach is summarized in a motto "Cool down, Slow down, and Engage constructively." Conflict competence is clearly for use *after* conflict has developed.

I have a different perspective. As I see it, what Kramer described as conflict competence is essentially the same thing I'm describing as a culture of collaboration, except that within my model, people like to strengthen their collaborative capacity and skills. As a result, they're willing to embed this collaborative model into conversations, as well as problem-solving and analysis. In contrast, they have no real intent to increase their conflict competence, except to have a check box in their profile to advance in their career. They are fearful of conflict, and they avoid it like it was a plague.

That same mindset is prevalent within the federal government of Canada's Informal Conflict Management System (ICMS). When I speak about fulfilling the mandate of managing conflict effectively by creating a culture of collaboration instead of developing conflict competence, some colleagues respond by referencing the legislative mandate of s. 207 of *The Public Service Modernization Act*,[21] which states:

> 207. *Subject to any policies established by the employer or any directives issued by it, every deputy head in the core public administration must, in consultation with bargaining agents representing employees in the portion of the core public administration for which he or she is deputy head, establish an informal conflict management system and inform the employees in that portion of its availability.*

The legislation speaks about a conflict management system. It doesn't prescribe how the system achieves effective conflict

---

21 The Public Service Modernization Act, *Statutes of Canada* (2003), c. 22, https://laws-lois.justice.gc.ca/eng/acts/p-33.4.

management. When we go to the policies, guess what we never see in any of them? "Conflict competence." Instead, we find references to a collaborative problem-solving model as a basis for conflict management. Here is one reference (and you will read other similar ones later in this book):

> ICMS: comprises a set of policies, procedures and structures that an organization integrates into its infrastructure to support a culture of effective conflict management and resolution using a collaborative problem-solving approach.[22]

The attachment to conflict and the hesitancy to disassociate from that label within this field of expertise is as counterproductive as it is real. The first documentation referencing a shift of focus from conflict to collaboration appears in the *ICMS Resource Guide*.[23] The text of that guideline was carefully crafted and approved by both labour and management. The existence of this language in that *Guide* is not an accident. I along with Thierry Casademont (a wonderful colleague) are its substantive authors. If you can access the *Guide*, you will note how the shift of focus "from illness to wellness" pervades that document.

It's the stigma associated with conflict that prevents broader use of any collaborative model, and unfortunately, some of the concepts around conflict resolution reinforce that stigma. The practice of conflict resolution has evolved upon a sound foundation. Confidentiality is often said to be a cornerstone. I get the positive side of that assurance. What about the negative side implicit in the *need* for confidentiality? I would suggest that the necessity of confidentiality[24] is akin to giving the assurance that no one will know you are in a conflict.

---

22   "ICMS for Departments," Treasury Board Secretariat (2018), accessed October 28, 2019, http://www.gcpedia.gc.ca/wiki/ICMS_-_For_Departments.

23   "ICMS Resource Guide," Treasury Board Secretariat (2017), accessed December 12, 2019, http://www.gcpedia.gc.ca/wiki/ICMS_-_For_Departments. (This document is embedded on that page.)

24   Other reasons for confidentiality might exist beyond protection of privacy. People do not want others to know they are in a conflict because conflict is judged negatively.

My Irish Catholic background leads me to draw an analogy to the confession of sins. Sins are commonly perceived as bad – just like the perception that conflict is bad. No Catholic has ever heard it said that there's a positive side to sin. No one has suggested that we can leverage sin. Nor that we can become "sin competent." I can't imagine that anyone would ever buy into that idea.

Let's look at some of the terms used for conflict resolution services. When conflict resolution experts work with groups, the service is typically called a "group intervention." What do you think it feels like to need an "intervention"? What does that message tell participants? Some of the tools in the field of conflict resolution also reinforce the stigma. How about a highly effective model of communication entitled "Nonviolent Communication"?[25] When we tell people that we offer non-violent communication training to address their conflicts, we're telling them that they're communicating violently now. In doing so, we are keeping the focus on illness.

Many conflict resolution service providers offer coaching – what kind of coaching? "Conflict coaching" of course.

Creative minds come up with creative titles for workshops:

- "Conflict Styles"
- "Profiting from Conflict"
- "Difficult Conversations"
- "Crucial Conversations"

These titles all convey negativity and complexity.

Confidentiality

Very often, especially early in the development of the practice of conflict resolution and mediation, the meetings happened at an off-site location. In part, that location was to emphasize neutrality and a balance of power. It also reinforced secrecy and confidentiality. Now,

---

25 Marshall B. Rosenberg, *Nonviolent Communication: A Language of Compassion* (San Diego, CA: Puddledancer Press, 2003). In his book, this American psychologist and mediator presents a model for communication which he entitled "nonviolent communication."

contrast that with a problem-solving session using the new collaborative model. Doesn't it seem far less likely that a need for confidentiality would arise? What if we set an objective to create widespread competence in collaboration? I think we can agree that most people would love to be better at collaboration. Would it ever occur to anyone to say that collaboration seems bad? Of course not. Therefore, we would openly hold the collaborative sessions in the workplace (unless more space was needed).

Neutrality

Neutrality is another cornerstone of conflict resolution. We know the two participants in a disagreement are not going to be neutral. So, if they aren't neutral, then who will be? If there is to be neutrality, then implicitly there must be the need for an expert facilitator/mediator/practitioner who exemplifies neutrality. And, if an expert is needed, then conflict and its resolution is obviously not simple. It is complex.

If a third person is required, then conflict resolution is beyond the ability of the participants to lead or manage as ordinary mortals. It must therefore be like an adjudicative process where you really need/should have a lawyer (except, perhaps, in smaller claims). Do lawyers help? Yes, they do – at several hundred dollars per hour. Sound reasons exist for certain elements of conflict resolution practice – that's not in question. The point is that despite those sound reasons, elements of practice and associated traditions reinforce the stigma that conflict is negative, thereby encouraging – unwittingly – avoidance.

In *Getting to Yes*, Fisher and Ury wrote in their acknowledgement:

> *Every day, families, neighbors, couples, employees, bosses, businesses, consumers, salesmen, lawyers, and nations face this same dilemma of how to get to yes without going to war. ... [W]e have evolved a practical method for negotiating agreement amicably without giving in* (Fisher and Ury, 1981, 4).

Fisher and Ury envisaged a simple process that anyone could apply to any disagreement in ordinary life. Their focus on international relations and their own scope of practice, as outlined in the "about the authors" portion, certainly recognizes the need for expertise. Their process of principled negotiations, though, was intended for everyday use. Their intent was to simplify negotiation (problem-solving), increase its effectiveness, and improve its outcomes (both for solutions and relationships). Wow, *how far* we have drifted from the initial thinking of Fisher and Ury!

Do you know what is really ironic? Schools are using this process that we've unwittingly chained to the negativity of conflict and enshrouded in complexity. Yes, in the school system, peer mediation programs exist. This came as a shock to me. I come from a professional background as a trial lawyer. As such, my thinking was that if there was potential for a lawsuit, then it was a situation for that TV warning: "Do not try this at home: call a professional." So, once trained as a mediator, I applied that same logic to this skill set. This made sense to me – especially since my training in conflict resolution was not really that much cheaper than my law degree!

My epiphany came when my younger son came home from school one day and announced that he had signed up for the peer mediation program. I thought it was cute. His dad was a mediator and he was going to be one at school! I stopped grinning and started thinking when he explained to me the process they were using, the steps he was following, and how he was doing it at school.

Then it occurred to me. If a school age student can learn a collaborative process and use it, then why can't adults? Why is it that if Paul and Kate are having a difficult relationship in British Columbia that I must fly from Prince Edward Island to help them? Why must they limit contact with each other until I get there to provide expert help? Instead, what if I coach them about how to use the collaborative model? What if I equip them with tools and skills to enable them to use my collaborative model in my absence?

But wait! If I can do that and they can use the collaborative model . . . what happens to me? Maybe Doug Hall is right – that people only listen to one radio station, WIIFM What's In It For Me (Hall, 2002, 41)?

I'm not suggesting for even one second that reinforcing the complexity of conflict is done as protectionism of self-interest for practitioners. What I'm wondering, though, is whether it's possible for conflict management practitioners (under whatever label), to entertain the idea of equipping others rather than delivering situational service directly.

My central point in this chapter is that, in creating and evolving this field of conflict resolution, practitioners did two things that continue to hinder the widespread use of any collaborative model:

1. We reinforced the stigma associated with conflict, thereby reducing the number of people who are exposed to collaborative processes.
2. We portrayed conflict as very complex and requiring experts. The adjudicative model more or less makes it essential to have experts like accountants and lawyers to argue the pros and cons of solutions to issues.

Collaboration and Competition

I want to touch upon the love of competition in western culture and perhaps in all of society. Some part of human nature is simply competitive. We learn about winning and losing early in life. We embed competition within our culture, not just in sports but also arts, education, commerce and employment. Competition is so tightly woven into our cultural fabric, we probably couldn't change that even if we wanted to – and we probably don't want to. Competition is healthy – well, healthy competition is. Most would agree that in general, competition is a good thing.

So, if we can't stop or don't want to stop competing, how can we stop conflict? We can't stop all conflict any more than we can stop all competition. That being said, we don't have to adopt a competitive approach to communication, problem-solving, or analysis, which is what the adjudicative model is, as our default. Nor do we have to dwell on conflict, fear it, or wait for it to escalate before we address it. Yet, that is exactly what most people do.

CHAPTER SEVEN
Avoidance and the Downward Spiral

The number one strategy for dealing with conflict is avoidance.

When conflict is avoided, relationships deteriorate and spiral downward in a very natural and normal way. Human nature seems to encourage us to fear things we don't understand and things we feel ill-equipped to address. Conflict is near the top of both of those lists for most people. As conflict escalates, it becomes less understood and increasingly challenging to address, which drives an increased sense of hopelessness, paralysis and avoidance.

Let's go back to the first point: *we naturally fear what we do not understand.* When the complexity and negativity of conflict is reinforced, talking about conflict being positive is a waste of good air. Rather than buying in, most people avoid addressing conflict in their relationships. When the avoidance strategy is used, the situation deteriorates: avoidance is *not* neutral.

On the next page is a visual depiction of the downward trajectory.

Downward Spiral of Unresolved Tension

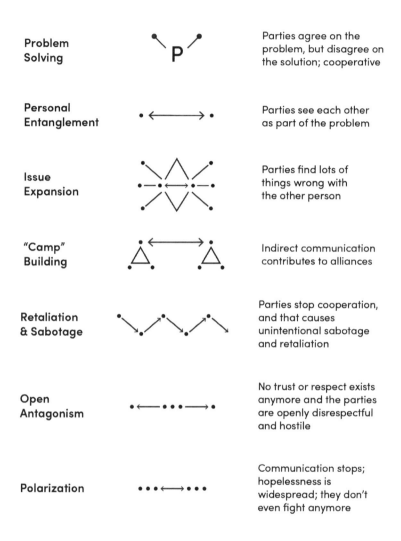

Problem Solving		Parties agree on the problem, but disagree on the solution; cooperative
Personal Entanglement		Parties see each other as part of the problem
Issue Expansion		Parties find lots of things wrong with the other person
"Camp" Building		Indirect communication contributes to alliances
Retaliation & Sabotage		Parties stop cooperation, and that causes unintentional sabotage and retaliation
Open Antagonism		No trust or respect exists anymore and the parties are openly disrespectful and hostile
Polarization		Communication stops; hopelessness is widespread; they don't even fight anymore

What follows is an explanation of each stage depicted in the diagram above. Let's bring back Paul and Kate for this illustration.

Stage One: Normal Problem-Solving

This represents normal problem-solving. Paul and Kate have different ideas, different perspectives, and different solutions to the problem being broached. At this point, they don't experience any tension, nor does either see the other as part of the problem.

Stage Two: Personal Entanglement

At this stage, either Paul or Kate begins to experience some level of tension about the other's approach to the problem and begins to associate that tension with the other person, associating them with the problem. It could be as simple as Paul thinking that Kate is too insistent on Kate's solution being the "right" solution. In short, Paul begins to perceive Kate as stubborn.

Stage Three: Issue Expansion

At this point, both Paul and Kate have some awareness of the tension between them. Once participants become a bit irritated with each other, it's natural to justify one's own reaction. A common way to do that is to notice other things that they do not like about the other person. So, Paul might notice that Kate is late for meetings (even if it happens rarely), or that Kate's clothing is either too stylish or too unprofessional. At the same time, Kate is making up her own list of pet peeves about Paul. Both are avoiding addressing the tension they are experiencing. Each is justifying their avoidance of the other by noticing additional little irritants.

Stage Four: Camp Building

Instead of addressing the rising tension, one or both begins (often mindlessly) to express frustration to those around them. Let's continue with Paul and Kate as the problem-solvers and add Sophie as their colleague. What Paul says to Sophie at this stage might sound something like "Sophie, have you ever worked with Kate? I like Kate, but . . . man, she can dig her heels in on an idea!" What is particularly damaging is that once the ball of criticism is set in motion, the momentum rapidly builds without anyone having to make any effort at all. Just watch it unfold.

Let's say that Sophie has to work with Kate on some file or situation, and Kate suggests a different solution than Sophie was proposing. What does Sophie naturally think? "Kate is stubborn, just like Paul said." And it continues. Let's say Sophie and Kate have a good relationship, and always greet each other with a big smile and a friendly hello. Paul and Sophie meet Kate in the hallway, just after Paul has expressed to Sophie his frustrations about Kate. Does Kate get the big smile and hello from Sophie? Not a chance. Instead Kate gets a muffled "hi," and wonders what has changed. Kate bumps into Nancy, another of their colleagues. She wonders aloud what's up with Sophie, noting that she has become very standoffish. Well, you can imagine the next time that Nancy meets Sophie who happens to be preoccupied with something and doesn't even notice Nancy! Without anyone's deliberate action, that ball of avoidance is accelerating down that slippery slope.

Stage Five: Retaliation and Sabotage

In stage five, the tension is mutual, and it is affecting other relationships. Suspicion serves to magnify unintentional mishaps and imports malicious intent where no ill will existed. Continuing with Paul and Kate, let's assume that Kate is supposed to do a piece of work that Paul needs and is expecting. In fulfillment of Murphy's Law, Kate innocently drops the ball. Paul, though, doesn't see it as innocent at all. And, the next time that Kate is expecting something from him, he responds in kind. "Tit for tat" becomes a game played more blatantly.

Stage Six: Open Antagonism

At a certain point, no one is playing innocent anymore. The relationship has become openly hostile and disrespectful. The whole group is divided into camps. Emotions are pretty raw. Every innocent omission is perceived as intentional. "If you're not with us, you're against us" is the mantra of the office. Cliques are widespread.

Stage Seven: Polarization

After a period of open hostility, the emotional responses subside. Neither Paul nor Kate cares enough to fight. Hopelessness is widespread. At this point, on the surface, their polarized workplace appears calm and even cooperative. Smaller subgroups splinter off to re-start the downward spiral within the cliques. "You cannot tick me off anymore because you are dead to me" is the mood of the polarized office.

Lessons from the Downward Spiral

As you were reading, did you recognize this stressful pattern of relationship deterioration, either as something you have heard about, witnessed, or experienced? When I pose that question in workshops, I see in people's eyes a sad acknowledgement of the reality that the spiral represents. That pattern is evident not just in bilateral relationships, but also in workplaces.

So, what can we take from this? I suggest three things:

1. Polarized relationships often begin as normal problem-solving.
2. Avoidance is *not* neutral.
3. Participants could choose to use collaborative communication and problem-solving processes at any stage.

What does this say about conflict resolution? I suggest three more things:

1. Most people don't use conflict resolution except as a last resort.
2. Avoidance is instinctive for many. It is a path of least resistance, taken by most.
3. Being collaborative/using collaborative processes is a **choice.**

This avoidant tendency acknowledges the truth that conflict is messy. No one wants to be involved in it, and very few know how to address conflict effectively (i.e., collaboratively). Obviously, the later the use of collaborative processes, the more difficult they are to use and the less likely they are to be successful. The human tendency toward avoidance is a key driver of the need to create a culture of collaboration.

CHAPTER EIGHT

Formal Processes to Treat Workplace "Illness"

The Canadian federal government's efforts demonstrate how counterproductive it is to focus on workplace illness. In the late 1980s to early 1990s, workplace tension was rising in offices across the federal government. The buzz word to describe it was "harassment." To address the situation, the government adopted a zero-tolerance policy on harassment.[26] When anyone felt harassed, they could bring a formal complaint. The complaint could trigger an investigation. The investigation would result in a report in which the complainant and respondent could see what others in the workplace said about the situation (and about them!). In a small percentage of cases, the complaint was upheld. Even in those cases, the workplace tension usually continued, in part because an investigative report created camps in the recount of the evidence gathered. In the larger percentage where the complaint was dismissed, the aftermath was even worse. The complainant typically felt victimized or re-victimized and the respondent (especially managers) felt attacked and abandoned by senior management. Others in the workplace felt that they were forced to choose sides. The "cure" was worse than the illness.

Soon after, the thinking shifted from investigation as the primary resolution mechanism, to the use of informal conflict resolution. Government adopted a policy on *early* conflict resolution, and informal resolution processes like mediation were offered to complainants and respondents in harassment cases. Where mediation was used, the complaints were successfully resolved in about 85 percent of cases.

---

26 "Policy on the Prevention and Resolution of Harassment in the Workplace," Treasury Board Secretariat (2001), accessed July 31, 2019, https://www.tbs-sct.gc.ca/pol/doc-eng.aspx?id=12414.

A significant problem remained, though, in that many cases didn't proceed to mediation. In those, the investigation had its usual impact.

In one department, we delivered information sessions about the policy on harassment and informal conflict resolution. As part of those sessions, one half of the participants made a list of the physical and emotional responses that they associated with being harassed. The other half of the participants made a list of those responses associated with being in a conflict. When we placed the flip charts side by side for the two groups, the participants noted that they had developed incredibly similar lists. The similarity of the impacts and experiences for each was making it difficult to distinguish harassment from conflict.

We presented conflict resolution processes like mediation as constructive ways to leverage the "positive side" of conflict. Despite our efforts, the volumes of complaints continued, and we had a minimal impact. The use of our "Office of Early Conflict Resolution" continued to be infrequent – so infrequent that my colleague joked that we were the "Office of Last Resort." Despite our using the sales pitch about a positive side of conflict, avoidance remained the most popular strategy for dealing with conflict and harassment. Conclusion? Keeping the focus on illness didn't work.

In 2005 as part of modernization of human resources legislation, the government introduced a requirement for departments to establish an informal conflict management system,[27] in essence, a mandated version of the early conflict resolution policy. The ICMS services are available across all government departments. These offices are well staffed with highly trained professionals. The services are free and confidential. No matter how you define success, for more than a decade in about 85 percent of situations where conflict resolution processes have been used, a consistent "improvement" has resulted. During that decade, mediator training has strengthened and mediators have expanded their skills and techniques. Therefore, the 85 percent cited is probably a low estimate.

---

27 The Public Service Modernization Act, *Statutes of Canada* (2003), c. 22, https://laws-lois.justice.gc.ca/eng/acts/p-33.4.

The cost effectiveness of a mediated versus an adjudicated solution is undeniable and widely known. Confidentiality for participants and neutrality of practitioners is broadly assured. Practitioners are highly trained and very skilled. Their success rate mirrors that of the mediators in the private sector. Typically, no costs were charged back to the local manager's budget and none at all were borne by the participants.

Notwithstanding the obvious advantages of the mediation process, a sharp increase in its utilization didn't happen. The use of informal conflict management system (ICMS) services only has a penetration rate of about 3 percent within the federal public service.[28] As noted earlier, although far more than 3 percent of the workforce participates in the Big Three conversations, only three percent are being reached by or reaching out to the ICMS. The point to be noted is that despite all of those promising steps and signs, the sharp increase in uptake didn't happen in the federal public sector either.

More recently, the "b" word (bullying) has been replacing the "h" word (harassment). A huge difference exists between the concept of conflict and those of bullying and harassment. A conflict tends to be seen as two-sided by most people. The old expression that "it takes two to tango" is mostly applicable to the breakdown in working relationships. The labels bullying and harassment, though, enable one participant to say that the relationship isn't working AND that the problem is *entirely* someone else's fault. While it is true that some situations of one-sided behaviour do occur – like harassment and bullying – these situations happen far less frequently than alleged.

Quite apart from frequency of occurrence and the concern that certain labels permit one person to place all responsibility upon the other, the focus on workplace dysfunction and illness isn't working, no matter what label is used.

---

28 "Annual Report ICMS Network 2014-16," Informal Conflict Management Network, (unpublished).

CHAPTER NINE

Conflict or Collaboration? Illness or Wellness? Heads or Tails?

Have you ever done a simple Google search for definitions of conflict? When I did that, I found that the depth of analysis and the level of dissection were overwhelming. On a quick read, conflict is dissected into constructive and destructive types; it's defined within a geo-political framework; its numerous gradations are elaborated upon; its relationship to other concepts like "dispute" and "differences" has been expounded upon. For philosophers, theorists, and academics, such dissection and analysis has value. For the ordinary person in daily life, though, those fine slices don't add up to much. If anything, the extra analysis complicates the matter reinforcing the complexity and mystery enshrouding conflict.

If we look for common denominators among the many definitions of conflict, we might see several. The term "differences" certainly appears frequently. As well, some psychological or emotional response is a common element. The most simplified definition, mentioned in chapter one, is this equation:

$$\text{Conflict} = \text{Problem} + \text{Tension}$$

Even if it's an oversimplification, this definition is useful to shift the focus from conflict to collaboration. This definition explains the universality of conflict; humans are natural problem-solvers. Solving problems is part of everyone's daily life. This definition also explains why not every difference is a "conflict" or a "dispute." We can have different perspectives about a solution to a problem – we frequently do – and we would never think of the situation as a conflict. The situation is just a normal problem, and the interaction is normal problem-solving as long as it's just a difference of perspectives.

The turning point from problem-solving to conflict is the introduction of a psychological or emotional response to the situation that indicates the beginning of tension. If we're discussing whether or not there is a conflict to be resolved, then we can argue about whether it's a conflict if only one person is experiencing tension. If we're debating whether the situation presents an opportunity for collaboration, then we don't need to discuss whether the emotional response is tension, the degree or quality of tension, or who is experiencing it.

The opportunity to be collaborative presents itself with each problem to be solved.

Therefore, as suggested earlier, we don't need to wait for a situation to merit the label "conflict" before we choose to be collaborative. I also expressed collaboration as an equation:

Collaboration = Better Solutions + Stronger Relationships

If conflict equals problem plus tension and collaboration equals better solutions plus stronger relationships, then conflict and collaboration may be viewed as opposite sides of the same coin. Where conflict is prevalent, problem-solving is difficult and relationships are tense; where collaboration is prevalent, people are developing better solutions and in doing so are strengthening their relationships, reducing tension, therefore reducing conflict, both in frequency and intensity.

The biggest problem with focusing on conflict resolution and conflict competence is inherently that when people use or develop either, they are doing so within the specific context of conflict itself. Outside of that context, how do they continue to analyze, communicate and problem-solve? By use of the adjudicative model. And, how did they end up in conflict? By use of the adjudicative model, of course!

To repeat the example I gave earlier, this is like the guy who suffers a heart attack, gets stabilized by adopting a healthy diet and exercise regime, and then returns to former bad habits that contributed to the heart attack in the first place. The "constructive" approach that he used to deal with the issue didn't change anything. When, I wonder, will we learn to abandon the focus on illness?

I love this analogy about being fixated on one mental model and not being able or willing to shift, used by Bob Chartier as a facilitator of National Management Community workshops. As I recall, he talks about the movie "Back to the Future 3." Marty (Michael J. Fox) takes a rifle back in time and happens upon a group trying to fend off a wild beast. Now, the group's mental model of dealing with wild animals is to throw things at it. Imagine that when Marty arrives, he tosses the rifle to someone in the group. What do they do with it? They throw it at the beast! Why? Because that's their mental model of handling a wild beast: throw things at it.

Do you think that earlier in history, when people hunted by throwing things at their prey, they had a label for how they hunted, or did they just call it hunting? If there is only one way to do something, it doesn't need a distinctive label – nothing exists as a contrast. When people problem-solve using the traditional method that I've labelled adjudicative, they don't call it "using the adjudicative model." They call it problem-solving and decision-making.

Well, problem-solving by the adjudicative model is today's equivalent to throwing things at prey, and in terms of efficiency, the collaborative model is the equivalent to firing the rifle to hunt instead. If we remain locked into the mental model of adjudication, then we can never use a collaborative model, not because using it is more difficult than using the adjudicative model: no, *people won't use it because they don't even know it exists.*

In the context of the federal government in Canada, a similar self-limiting mental model exists arising from the legislative term "informal **conflict** management system." That term keeps the focus on conflict as part of the mental model of the ICMS network. What if the best way to manage conflict is to embed collaborative skills and models within the fabric of the public service? What if embedding those elements of collaboration created a culture of collaboration where workplace tension levels are reduced? What if creating a culture of collaboration not only limited the incidence of conflict but also had numerous positive impacts on things like innovation and implementation of change?

Here's another analogy around mental models and how limiting they can be on our thinking. Consider a department of health or a hospital with a mandate to maintain a healthy population, or shall we say, implement a health care management system. One way to do that is to focus on the treatment of illness; another is to focus on wellness. Either focus has the potential to be an effective health care management system. When the focus is on addressing illness, some effort is also expended on encouraging wellness. If the system focuses on wellness, it still provides services to address illness. All the eggs are never in one basket only. In that same way, a conflict management system can strengthen the health of the workplace by focusing on conflict, or it can do so by focusing on collaboration. Again, in either case, efforts and services are expended on both targets. The choice of primary focus, though, isn't controlled by the legislative wording. The choice of focus should be based on what will most likely accomplish the objective or mission intended. If that choice requires the adoption of a new mental model, then so be it.

I mentioned earlier that several links exist between ICMS and a collaborative approach, and here are a few more:

> *informal resolution process*
>
> *a confidential and voluntary collaborative problem-solving approach such as face to face conversation, conflict coaching, facilitated discussion or mediation that has the advantage of addressing the parties' needs, concerns and mutual interests. Informal resolution processes are also commonly called interest based conflict resolution, Informal Conflict Management System (ICMS) and alternative dispute resolution.*[29]

Within the policy structure around the ICMS, these phrases appear:

- *It is a system that supports a culture of effective conflict management that emphasizes honest discussion and collaborative problem-solving between people who are involved in conflicts.*
- *Talented employees will remain in an organization that is respectful of its people, gives them avenues to voice their concerns*

---

29 "Policy on Harassment Prevention and Resolution," Treasury Board Secretariat (2012), accessed July 31, 2019, http://www.tbs-sct.gc.ca/pol/doc-eng.aspx?id=26041. See Appendix A of the policy.

safely, allows them to grow in an inclusive and collaborative workplace . . .
- *An ICMS is a system approach to dealing with workplace conflicts. It is composed of the following functions:*
    - *informal processes*
    - *conflict management training.*
- *These functions are designed to support a culture of effective conflict management and resolution using a collaborative problem-solving approach.*
- *ICMS: comprises a set of policies, procedures and structures that an organization integrates into its infrastructure to support a culture of effective conflict management and resolution using a collaborative problem-solving approach.*[30]

The Department of Justice ICMS program evaluation[31] states:

> *Although some progress has been made, it is unreasonable to have expected that a significant shift towards a collaborative workplace culture would have occurred given the size of the Department and the comparatively small size and scope of the program.*

To create a supportive engaging workplace, we need to shift focus from illness to wellness, from developing conflict competence to creating a culture of collaboration. In my vision of a culture of collaboration, this collaborative model is embedded within communication and problem-solving. Consequently, less tension arises and when it does, it is more easily addressed. And, it follows that fewer situations of conflict, harassment, and bullying will arise.

What those excerpts above demonstrate is the close connection between addressing conflict and increasing collaboration. The

---

30　"A Guide to the Key Elements of an ICMS in the core Public Administration," Treasury Board Secretariat (2008), accessed April 28, 2019, https://www.canada.ca/en/treasury-board-secretariat/services/healthy-workplace/informal-conflict-management-system/guide-key-elements-icms-core-public-administration.html.

31　"Informal Conflict Management System Evaluation," Department of Justice (2015), accessed October 26, 2019, http://www.justice.gc.ca/eng/rp-pr/cp-pm/eval/rep-rap/11/icm s-sgice/p3.html.

difference is one of focus: Conflict or collaboration. Illness or wellness. Heads or tails. Opposite sides of the same coin. One side is the negative, the other is the positive.

CHAPTER TEN

The New Collaborative Model – Applying the 6 Steps

In Chapter Two, I introduced a new collaborative model, describing what each step accomplishes. In this chapter, I will share more information about what is happening at each step and why each step is so important. This information will give you a better understanding of how this collaborative model can be used for communication, problem-solving, and analysis.

To reiterate, the six steps of this collaborative model are:

1. Set Parameters
2. Exchange Perspectives
3. Describe Issues
4. Identify Interests
5. Generate Options
6. Select Solutions

Set Parameters

The *Set Parameters* step involves talking about how we're going to talk about what we're going to talk about, before we talk about the merits or subject matter itself. In the field of conflict resolution, there are a couple of extremes. At the more directive, the facilitator/mediator states a set of "ground rules" about what conduct and behaviours are expected and what will not be permitted during the conversation. At the more permissive, the facilitator will ask the participants how they want to have the conversation and will invite the participants to speak up when they feel that the agreed upon parameters aren't being respected. At that point, the facilitator will engage the participants in a conversation about how they want to move forward.

If you Google opening statements for mediators (please do), you will be absolutely confused by the contrast between what I'm describing and what "experts" are providing as classic "tried and true" opening statements. Those suggested statements would make it seem that the purpose of the introductory stage is to build the mediator's credibility with the participants. Some even sound like the mediator hasn't done any preparatory meetings with participants, and almost all of them sound like the whole process is entirely focused on reaching a settlement. Just because someone mediates doesn't mean they are using the collaborative model: they can use an adjudicative model and simply facilitate the dialogue leading to the parties agreeing upon some middle ground. That facilitation can happen without regard to their underlying interests and without any improvement to relationships, simply by focusing on bridging the gap between two positions (i.e., the facilitation of an adjudicative model).

Even if you are in the field of conflict resolution, try to think of the *Set Parameters* step as a broader stage than an introduction designed for getting people comfortable in the room. There's a strong evidentiary basis for setting parameters for the conversation before entering into the subject matter. In order to explain the significance of this step, I need to bring in the work of the Gottman Institute, and its study of relationships, which I will reference in greater detail later. The Gottmans – John and Julie – are two psychologists who studied the relationship of marriage for over forty years. Their research environment was dubbed the "love lab." The "lab" consisted of a kitchenette, dining room set, and a sofa. Couples would come into the lab and have conversations about everything under the sun: children, finances, work, sex, friends, infidelity – nothing was off limits.

The conversations were observed, recorded, and analyzed by the scientists looking for patterns for good and bad outcomes. The Gottman team gleaned from the evidence they collected very early on, that they could predict whether the conversation would end well or not, irrespective of the subject matter. Their research demonstrated an ability to predict success or failure with a 95 percent accuracy rate based on what happened in the first three minutes. Those couples likely to be successful took the time to talk about *how* they were going to talk about *what* they were going to talk about, before they got into the subject matter. In essence, they set the parameters for how they were going to communicate. Doing so created a positive atmosphere of safety and cooperation, and reduced the instances of criticism, blame, and therefore defensiveness, when the controversial portions of the conversations began.

Set Parameters is therefore a key step in any collaborative model. Often, and especially in an adjudicative model, zero time is spent discussing how a conversation will happen. People just jump in and the "argument-counter argument" cycle begins immediately and continues until some wrap up happens. Frankly, many of those "model opening statements" on the internet don't make even a shallow effort to set parameters for the participants to engage. That's a huge opportunity missed.

When I'm working as a facilitator/mediator with people, I tell them that we're going to spend the first ten minutes talking about how they are going to talk about what they came to talk about. What I do is simply ask them to tell me what completes this statement for them: "What I need in order to have a safe and productive conversation is . . . " Then, I wait through their silence until someone speaks (usually that's no more than a minute, although the first few times, it felt like an hour!).

So, let's assume that without the presence of a mediator, two people are sitting down to have a conversation about a touchy subject and they want to use this new collaborative model. They don't need a facilitator to pose that same question, do they? Doesn't it work just as well if one of them says "Before we get into the merits of our views, since we know this is a bit touchy for us, how about we take a few minutes to talk about how we want to have a productive discussion?" Based on the Gottman research, even if that was the only thing people did differently, they would significantly increase their chances of having a successful outcome to their conversations. Obviously, in a culture of collaboration, taking that time at the outset would be the norm, not the exception.

Exchange Perspectives

The *Exchange Perspectives* step is fundamentally different from people making opening statements to outline their opposing positions and supporting rationales to start the debate, like in the adjudicative model. When a person states their position and rationale, it's all but explicit that their position is "right," and therefore the other's position is wrong. If one party states their version of past events instead of a position, it's equally clear that for that party, their version is the "truth" and that the other party is mistaken at best, lying at worst. That type of approach cannot do other than to express blame and criticism, and therefore will almost always trigger a defensive response, either as a counter-attacking criticism or a defence to excuse themselves. Remember that the adjudicative model is about deciding/ persuading which choice is the right decision; it's all or nothing. So, if you are not right, you are wrong. Things are either fact or fiction, true or false. No room exists for "alternative facts."

In this collaborative model, the point of departure is recognition that the participants' views are simply perspectives. I strongly encourage the use of the word "perspective." An opening preface like "I have a different perspective" conveys a far different message than the classic type of opening to a debate. Expressing one's viewpoint as a perspective increases the likelihood that the other person is going to hear what is said.

What we think is fact is often inter-twined with assumptions. People say we shouldn't make assumptions. Yet we must make some assumptions in order to make sense of the world around us by filling in information gaps. In most interactions between two people, each person has only two of three key pieces of information. Let's return to Paul and Kate as an example:

- Paul has his intention and the actions he takes to achieve his intent
- Kate has her experience, i.e., her observations of Paul's actions, and how she has been affected by them

In order to make sense of their experience, Kate needs to make an assumption about Paul's intent. If Kate's experience is negative, then it makes sense to her that Paul must have intended that. Paul can't know the impact of his actions on Kate, and assumes that the impact is consistent with what he intended. He has to make the assumption that his impact on Kate will be positive, or at least neutral. In other words, if Paul had known his actions would not have achieved his intent, then he would have chosen different ones.

When tension rises, each forgets that they made assumptions and tends to express their assumptions as if they were absolute fact and truth. Often, people are very confident that their assumptions are accurate, and in reality, their assumptions are very often quite far off.

When Kate accuses Paul of mal-intent, Paul becomes defensive. When Paul expresses disbelief about Kate's description of how she was impacted, Kate becomes even more wounded. Only Paul knows Paul's intent and only Kate knows Kate's experience. If, on the other hand, Kate speaks about impact and Paul speaks of intent, neither can quibble because each is talking about what only they know for sure. None of that content can provoke defensiveness. In the exchange of perspectives, when a participant describes how they've been impacted without attacking the other participant's motives, the perspective is more easily heard without defensiveness.

Above, I said that this step is about the opportunity to both hear and to be heard. It's helpful when using this collaborative model to be very transparent about these dual objectives. If two people are both going to have that chance, then it matters far less who goes first. In an adjudicative debate model, the second person speaking is responding and rebutting the comments of the first person, whereas in this collaborative model, the second person is simply sharing a different view of the situation, saying essentially what they would've said had they spoken first.

At the end of the exchange of perspectives, each should sense that they've been heard and are understood. As well, they should be able to put together a short starting list of what they want, and what they want to avoid, in any outcome or decision. During the exchange, it's common to hear the seeds of options that could be explored, and it is a good idea to note these so as not to lose sight of them. Each should have a clear understanding of at least their own main theme, and ideally, that of the other as well. This will serve them well in step three.

Collaborative Listening – Dramatically Different

Switching to the opportunity to hear, the listening process in this new collaborative model is distinctly different from an adjudicative one. In an adjudicative model, the idea is to respond with a counter argument. Therefore, the most effective listening style for *that* model is "listen to respond." In this collaborative model, people use a "listen to learn" approach. This requires a spirit of curiosity, openness to the idea that the other perspective is *different* rather than *wrong*. I often say that even the criminally insane have a reason for what they do – it makes sense to them. In this new collaborative model, the point of listening is to figure out how the other's perspective makes sense to *them*.

Listening to learn is a skill, not just a concept, and like any skill it needs practice. Studies suggest that we can speak at about 150 words per minute and can absorb about 450 words per minute.[32] Therefore, we have additional processing capacity in our brains when we are listening to someone. The natural inclination is to use that capacity to process a response, hence the tendency is to listen to respond instead of listen to learn.

In a collaborative conversation, that additional capacity can be put to excellent use. Remember those underlying interests that inform a person's perspective? The person listening can make some hunches about those, making either mental or written notes about what they think is important to the other person, and driving their perspective, including what they either want or want to avoid.

Rather than posing questions to pin the speaker, the listener can use expanding questions to explore the perspective that they are hearing. "Can you tell me more about that?" "Can you help me understand

32   Laura Janusik, "Listening Facts," *International Listening Association*, accessed October 26, 2019, https://www.listen.org/Listening-Facts.

how that would work?" "What do you think is the important objective that is supported by what you're saying?"

Another good use of that surplus processing power is to formulate a paraphrase of what is being heard, firstly to ensure that the message being received is what the speaker intends, and secondly, to communicate that the listener understands the speaker's perspective, especially if the listener has a drastically different view.

Note how the impact is significantly different in the effort to express understanding of the other's perspective in a collaborative model than in an adjudicative one. In the adjudicative model, the effort to express understanding is reflected far too often with these starting words: "I understand what you're saying, but . . . "

Describe Issues

The *Describe Issues* step is a joint effort, set up by the listening in step two. Either or both may take a stab at the whole issue, or at their own theme, or at that of the other. To the extent they try to express the other's theme, they are demonstrating appreciation of each other. Later on, I will come back to why that's so important. Verner Smitheram, former Director of the Studies in Conflict Resolution program at University of Prince Edward Island, used to say that framing the issues was to ask the question "What do you need to fix in order to leave here with a successful outcome?" As you can see, Verner's formulation is very problem-solving oriented, at least in its appearance. Gordon Sloan,[33] who is also a trainer, spoke about framing the issue as opening the umbrella. If the issue isn't acceptable to both on first try, open the umbrella wider.

You may wonder how broad it can be. The answer is that it can be as broad as it needs to be; and, it can be a blend between task and relationship orientations, or focused on either as needed. I have worked with participants where the acceptable issue was "How do we strengthen our working relationship?" and with others where the

---

33 Gordon Sloan is a well-known mediator and instructor residing in British Columbia, Canada, with whom I took several training workshops.

issue was acceptably framed for them as "How do we succeed on this project together?" No matter how the issue is stated, the important things are:

- Each person can see their perspective within it, with room to talk about what they want to talk about.
- The language is non-judgmental, non-blaming, and balanced.
- It gives each participant the opportunity to address the heart of the matter, as they perceive it.

Remember that a perfectly acceptable outcome of a collaborative conversation is to agree to disagree, to be okay with no solution, and be content instead with simply an increased appreciation of the other's perspective. Rome wasn't built in a day. Comprehensive solutions aren't often built in ten minutes or an hour. By contrast, mutual appreciation *can* grow in that timeframe, using a collaborative model of communicating and problem-solving.

The temptation to jump to solutions is a common pitfall at this point. Framing the issue so that it doesn't suggest a solution reduces that risk. Because we're rational creatures and therefore natural problem-solvers, it's tempting to conceive a simple solution to a complex problem. Please don't skip steps. Follow the model. Trust it.

Identify Interests

In this collaborative model, the participants already have a head start on the *Identify Interests* step. Those mini-lists created during the exchange of perspectives can be placed on a sheet to be used for tracking during the *Identify Interests* step. Continuing with Paul and Kate, they could start with a sheet that looks like this:

Paul	Wants	Kate
	Want to Avoid	

One might say that the interests are a paraphrase, in one or two words, of a perspective or a position. The "interest" phrase really is one or two words that describe the criteria for a good solution to the issue being discussed. It's important that interests aren't solutions themselves – those belong on the options list that will be generated at step five.

The things that don't easily lend themselves to a positive expression or phrase go under the "Want to Avoid" category, always the shorter list. The insertion of the mini-list from the exchange of perspectives enhances the positive atmosphere. Whereas at the *Exchange Perspectives* step, the level of appreciation of each other's views is at a surface level only, this step deepens that base. Quite casually, the participants go back and forth with exploring expanding questions, learning more about how the other sees the situation. Either each for themselves, for each other or together, they identify the underlying interests at play. If we were to think back to Paul and Kate and to picture them identifying interests at this stage, Paul might say: "What I think should happen is we each take five minutes to explain our ideas before we start thinking about making any decision. As I think about what I want, if I were expressing it as an interest, I think my interest is being heard."

Once the participants believe they've exhausted this exercise, they move to *Generate Options* knowing that they can come back to *Identify Interests* at any time. Later in this section, I will write about how the model has checks and balances to ensure that something important isn't overlooked.

One of the concerns about the principled negotiation model was that it could enable the "hard bargainer" to gain too much information and manipulate a situation. Could this also happen with this collaborative model? Did that cross your mind especially around the listing of things you want to avoid? Here are some observations from my experience, which may provide some comfort:

- It is an exchange of thoughts and exploration of interests. If one perceived it to be one-sided, then it would seem appropriate to pause or proceed with some caution, so as not to develop vulnerability.
- This isn't an exposure of weakness of positions, it's a list of things that would be impacted by ideal solutions.
- If the other participant is thinking about how to satisfy what is important to you, even with the goal of taking advantage of you, then that is probably a good thing because they are thinking about how your interests can be met.

Generate Options

Earlier, I wrote that the participants generate new ideas by asking themselves: "What could we do to resolve the issues we are working on in ways that would satisfy our interests?" And, I stated that the key to this step is to avoid early evaluation of options. You will recall that in an adjudicative model, each option is evaluated and critiqued as it arises. That early evaluation kills creativity, because people don't like their ideas and thoughts being judged.

In this collaborative model, a simple rule is made explicit and followed without exception. In order to avoid early evaluation, the participants explicitly agree that they will not at this point explain, clarify, justify or defend the options they propose. Each idea is presented in a "twenty words or less" statement. What if you need to know more? Wait. What if the idea seems stupid? Wait. What if you have a "but what if . . . " question? Wait. You will have that chance. It's just a question of timing, and the delayed timing is important if you want to be creative, collaborative, and to search for the optimal solution.

Any number of creativity techniques can be used here. The one I would strongly recommend against is the "Six Hats."[34] That technique necessarily involves early evaluation. I like techniques that leverage different participants' learning and thinking styles, and which support introverts and extroverts. For me, I often write to think. A brilliant colleague of mine in the practise of law was a doodler, and he drew all kinds of things as a mechanism to aid his thinking. (I expect he continued to do that when lawyers were presenting arguments to him when he became a judge.) The bottom line is that people can use whatever works for them. I encourage experimentation because like Einstein said, "If we do what we always did, we will get what we always got." I also encourage diversity of techniques and stimuli because of the evidence gathered at Doug Hall's *Eureka Ranch*™ (Hall, 2002).

One of the stimuli available to participants is their list of interests just created. There are two ways to use this list – one optional and one very important. The optional one is to ask, one interest at a time, how it could be addressed. That is methodical and not necessarily very conducive to creativity. The highly-suggested one comes at the end of the *Generate Options* step, otherwise called brainstorming. It is good

---

34 Edward De Bono, *Six Thinking Hats: An Essential Approach to Business Management* (Boston: Little, Brown, 1985). In this text, Edward De Bono explains this parallel thinking technique providing a structure to explore six distinct perspectives of a complex issue or scenario.

practice to go back over the list of interests and ensure that at least one option exists to address each interest. Remember above where I said the model has check points to show if you missed something? This is one of those built-in check points: is there at least one option for every interest identified?

Select Solutions

Finally, when the participants have exhausted their creative efforts, they are at *Select Solutions*. Earlier I wrote that the selection is essentially accomplished by the participants asking themselves this question: "Which of the options generated best address the issues we are working on in a way that satisfies the interests we listed?" While overall, that question will get to the outcome, there are a few tips to make it easier.

When I work with people as a facilitator of a collaborative process, I list their options on a flip chart. On that chart, I leave a space to the left of the list of options generated. The more people, the bigger the space I leave. I use that space in *Select Solutions* to mark whether they think the idea is high, medium, or low for them as a solution. I note their response as "H", "M", or "L." Any two people having a collaborative conversation to address issues can also leave some space to the left on the list of their ideas and use it in that same way.

Here's another tip that helps people to be effective at *Select Solutions*. Do the high, medium, or low ranking without any discussion, explanation, or justification about the ranking each assigns. That is, if Paul says the first idea is a high for him, and Kate thinks it's a low for her, they don't have the conversation *at that moment* about why they ranked the idea differently. They rank all the ideas first. So, they have a parameter in place for this step, where they agree not to explore at this moment beyond answering the question, "Is this idea a High, Medium, or Low?" A deeper discussion of different ratings will happen after all ideas have been ranked.

The value of that ban on early discussions becomes apparent in this example when the ranking is complete. Let's assume Paul and Kate have fifteen options on their list. In using the H/M/L technique, typically, it results in about six marked H by both, three marked L by both, three more with close rankings. Lastly, there are three where one thinks the options are high and the other thinks they are low. Without doing anything else, Paul and Kate know that they have the basis of a solution. In using this ranking technique, they also avoid being tempted to revert to positions over differences that are typically more imaginary than real. The technique also illustrates where real differences exist, in those ranked H by one and L by the other.

So, what do they do with these differences? They have a conversation that starts with, "What is it about this option that makes it a low (or high) for you?" They explore their perspectives to determine what interest underlies their ratings. Often it turns out that the difference in rating is resolved simply by exchanging perspectives – after listening, one person or the other gains a new appreciation of the option, sees it differently, and changes their rating. In other cases, though, this exploration serves as a second check point to ensure interests aren't missed and to revisit a step if they were. When an interest is missed, the participants do a mini-step five to figure out what they could do with either a new option or a modified existing option to ensure all of their interests are addressed. In some cases, the interests can't be addressed and the participants either accept that as an indefinite status or as something to be revisited.

High Five Technique

For groups larger than about five, I use a "high five" technique rather than the H/M/L one. You may see this on an internet search referred to as the "fist of five." Perhaps I'm just too positive – I prefer to label it the "high five." In this technique, as the facilitator, I give the explanation as follows:

> *We are going to do a quick poll to see how close we are to consensus on several of these options. It will be a show of fingers, not hands. Five fingers means you love the idea – wish it was yours. Four means you are very content with it. Three means you can live with it, even if you prefer*

a different idea. Two means you have serious concerns about this idea. One means you cannot live with it.

Similar to the H/M/L technique, the idea is to move through every option, before having further discussion on any of them. I note the ones and twos for each. Again, I'm likely to end up with a series of options where the popular response is fours and fives, some as mainly threes, and some that only a few see as a one or a two. From that point, I do mini-discussions, exploring the perspectives driving the one and two finger votes where most have voted with fours and fives. Sometimes, the larger group changes, other times, the smaller one does. In still other cases, the group recognizes that important interests have been overlooked and either new or improved solutions are generated.

You may have heard of a technique called "dot-mocracy" where group participants are given the same number of dots, perhaps of three colours where each has a weight (1, 2, 3, etc.) The participants place these beside their top choices. Dot-mocracy merits a note of caution. Some evidence exists that in hierarchical groups at least, this technique may produce skewed results because some participants may want to appear as associating with the ideas of certain others.[35] A way to avoid that would be to number the ideas, and have participants write their top three on a slip of paper, which are then collected and posted accordingly, or exchanged and posted.

Trust, Good Faith, Compliance, Accommodation, and the "Hard Bargainer"

These five topics are the poster concepts for why it is said by some that a collaborative approach won't work. There has to be trust in order to have collaboration, they say. People have to have an assurance that each participant will exercise good faith, they say. Mediated

35 Len Fisher, *The Perfect Swarm: the Science of Complexity in Everyday Life* (New York: Basic Books, 2009) 93-101. Fisher notes the importance of independent thinking in any voting system. A hierarchical structure would likely limit that freedom of thought giving potential space for the "groupthink" phenomenon or a "follow the leader" approach to voting.

agreements don't work because there is no stick to ensure compliance, they say. And finally, they say that if people try to be collaborative, then they will give up or give in to the hard bargainer, sacrificing their own interests in order to preserve a relationship.

I will start by saying I've never facilitated a mediation where participants had a high level of trust about the other. The norm is that each side asserts their own good faith and worries about that of the other participant. If we look back to the diagram with the downward spiral, at what stage would we find trust? I suggest you would find trust primarily at the stage of normal problem-solving. From personal entanglement downward, trust decreases. Trust and good faith are closely connected; if one is decreasing, the other is too. How do I address that? I tell participants that I expect them to be sceptical and pessimistic about whether any progress can be made, and that their scepticism is their way of protecting themselves. Lastly, I tell them that it's my job to be the optimist.

As I mentioned earlier, 85 percent of mediations are successful. In the other 15 percent (the unsuccessful ones), the lack of success isn't related to an absence of trust and good faith in my experience. Sometimes, the timing isn't conducive. Other times, outside forces and influences discourage participation to the end. In a few cases, new information comes to light. In still others, where perhaps both parties initially thought that an agreement would be adequate, a principle surprisingly gained prominence where either or both recognized that they would be better served by an adjudicative solution – a binding ruling. Returning to the 85 percent of mediations that arrive at a resolution, and assuming that participants started without trust or confidence about the good faith of the other, what can we conclude? I conclude that trust is not a prerequisite to embarking on a collaborative process.

The concern about compliance and the risk of being overly-accommodating deserve examination as well. Both of these concerns are satisfied by re-examining the process, wherein each side identifies what they want, and what they want to avoid. Together, they generate options that might address those key interests. When they select solutions, each does so because the option selected meets their *own* needs. It happens that the solution also may serve compatible interests of the other participant. Continuing with Paul and Kate, the fact that an option serves Kate's interests isn't why Paul rates an option as high. Paul rates it as high because his own interests are being served. In preparation I tell each participant that to my mind, there's only one reason for them to enter an agreement: it serves that participant's own interests. And, I ask them, as I am asking you to consider this: if Kate enters an agreement because the terms within it meet her interests, then does Paul have to worry about Kate's follow through or compliance?

In the agreement itself, if I'm preparing it with them, I capture what issues they wanted to address, and what each wanted/wanted to avoid; I then list the options that they considered and/or chose. I confirm with them that they're choosing those solutions because the solutions serve their interests and, I add an explicit statement to that effect. The accommodator style actually benefits from the collaborative model because it keeps them focused on both task and relationship, not just the latter as would be their norm, especially when pressed in an adjudicative-based conversation. Lastly on this point, a mediated agreement isn't any less enforceable than any other agreement to resolve issues.

What about the "hard bargainer"? Can collaborative processes work with them? The short answer is sometimes yes, and sometimes no. Hard bargainers share the same universal core concerns that I mention later. While hard bargainers may be more focussed on task than relationship in their communication and problem-solving styles, they will still have some relationship interests as well. On that basis alone, I would ask: what's there to lose by attempting to use a collaborative approach? If collaboration isn't working and you want to change your approach, it's not like you have to cave before you switch. I invite people to think about how effectively the traditional adjudicative model has worked (or not!) with hard bargainers. My final question is, what risk is being mitigated by not attempting a collaborative process first?

Whether real or perceived, doesn't power imbalance as an objection to being collaborative resolve itself the same way? If Kate could do whatever she wanted simply on the basis of authority, then why would she not do so? More importantly, if Kate can do that, then how is Paul more vulnerable by engaging Kate in a collaborative conversation? Isn't Kate the one who may be vulnerable and change?

Group Use of This Model

Significant advantages exist with this collaborative model for group problem-solving. Firstly, it is probably far less open to "group think." A more valuable advantage, though, is its capacity to harness diversity and resistance. In this collaborative model, the process incorporates and reflects as many interests as possible to arrive at the best decision or solution. When groups use this collaborative model, they leverage diversity rather than dismiss it.

In the adjudicative model, once the decision is made, any interests arising from perspectives that are different from the majority view are not reflected in, or served by, the option chosen by the majority. I mentioned above that often groups lose valuable talent because some participants experience their voices being unheard at best, dismissed at worst. When those members leave, sometimes they offer their talents to other groups. Other times, they become extra casualties of the adjudicative model – talent wasted.

In an adjudicative model, resistance to the majority view is perceived as a negative force to be overcome. In that model, the majority expends a significant amount of energy on "managing" resistance, especially during the implementation of change. The key strategies for managing resistance are isolation and marginalization of those showing resistance which is a total waste of their talent.

This collaborative model, on the other hand, leverages resistance. It's true that the resistant people aren't great cheerleaders during a creativity session. Their negativity toward the majority view doesn't create any warmth in the room at the *Exchange Perspectives* step either. The resistant ones do add value though at the *Select Solutions* stage and during implementation. If listened to, those resisting because they are pointing out weaknesses will serve to strengthen the solutions being chosen. Looking at Rogers Curve of Adoption, the proportion of a group that is last to respond to change, the resistors, is normally quite small, 16 percent.[36] In a collaborative model, the majority expends energy exploring how resistors' ideas can be incorporated, either in refining the solution or in its implementation. By demonstrating appreciation of the key interests underlying the resistance and in incorporating those within the solution selected, the group leverages the resistance with far greater effectiveness than the majority manages it in the adjudicative model.

The Caution: Collaboration is Not a "One Size fits All" Solution

No solution, no rule, no process, is without exceptions. Seldom, if ever, does one size fit all. That proposition applies equally to the collaborative model I've described. Certain situations do lend themselves to appropriate and effective use of the adjudicative model. In the private sector particularly, it's often the case that the primary business owner both has a greater investment and is more informed than anyone else. In that circumstance, it may well be that a single individual possesses almost all of the knowledge in the room, and is often faced with a business crisis, usually arising from a change by competitors. In those circumstances, collaboration will probably take more time than is merited.

In the corporate world and within government, it's common to find strong attachment to the status quo. The challenge with addressing organizational inertia was probably a significant driver of the invention of the Agile and LEAN processes. As I understand Agile and LEAN, these innovation approaches attempt to break the situation down into easily manageable chunks and to deliver some minimal viable solution to begin progress. In setting the expectation that some viable change will result, these processes work against corporate inertia. In

---

36   The Rogers Adoption Curve is also known as the "Diffusion Process."

the absence of those kinds of processes, the adjudicative model is typically more effective than the collaborative model to address inertia.

That organizational inertia isn't easily addressed using either model actually. The collaborative model could be used by the historic majority in the enterprise to ensure that the group gets caught up in exploring endless possibilities or searching for perfection. Doing so would prevent any decision-making, thereby maintaining the status quo. The adjudicative model can be manipulated by early evaluation of ideas for change to bring the group to a "no" decision. That early evaluation can be based on challenges in implementation, business risk, growth-profitability analysis, or any of a hundred other good reasons. That said, the adjudicative model is probably a better tool for addressing inertia because the decision is framed as a choice between only two or three solutions, including a preferred solution. Quite frequently the adjudicative model presents the status quo as a poor option, which will lead to a decision to change even if the preferred option isn't an optimal one.

In both private and public sector, inexperience can be lethal. Any process, adjudicative or collaborative, is unlikely to mitigate against inexperience.

CHAPTER ELEVEN

The New Collaborative Model – For Communication, Problem-Solving, Analysis, and Decision-Making

For Communication – Monique and Juanita

Communication using an adjudicative model can produce disastrous consequences for relationships. I mentioned earlier the *Bottle*, the *Blurt*, and the *Blab*. Using a collaborative approach can repair the damage done from those conversations. Let me give you a real-life example.

In a fairly large production centre, Monique, a manager, was leading an operation of some 75 employees with five team leaders (TLs). Monique was a quiet introvert. One of the five, Juanita, had been hoping for a permanent role as a TL. When Juanita joined the team, Monique was concerned about rumours that Juanita wasn't good with sensitive information. Monique relied on some more experienced TLs instead, even for a few decisions that impacted Juanita's unit. Juanita was insecure and noticed that Monique spent more time with other TLs than with her. Monique wasn't generous with her praise and Juanita sensed she received very little. Juanita was a star in terms of performance. Despite that, she began to wonder what she needed to do to impress Monique. Sometimes, she wondered out loud. Sometimes, her frustration leaked into her conversations.

Monique didn't hear any of this directly, but she heard lots of it indirectly. She felt attacked and undermined, thinking that Juanita wanted to get rid of her. She was in an acting role as manager and was hoping to be made permanent. The higher pay was important to her. The instability that could result from Juanita's criticisms was a big threat. At the same time, Juanita was wondering if Monique was waiting her out so that her managerial assignment would end and she would be sent back to her former level.

Interestingly, both thought that the other was poisoning their reputation. Each wanted to quit; each went home sick on multiple occasions from the stress in the relationship. Their working relationship was becoming increasingly toxic.

Looking back on how they and the people around them communicated, it was obvious that the *Bottle*, the *Blurt*, and the *Blab* were engrained patterns in their workplace. Monique listened to the blabbing of others and pre-judged Juanita as unable to handle sensitive information. Therefore, Monique kept Juanita outside her inner circle.

Juanita wanted to be relied upon, to have influence, and to be included. Juanita bottled up her feelings of being excluded and isolated. No matter what Monique did, Juanita's pattern was to hear exactly what she feared she was going to hear from Monique. Juanita blabbed to other people about it being impossible to please Monique. Juanita feared failure. She expressed that she felt Monique was trying to get rid of her. She didn't even feel like coming to work. Her stress was enormous; her health was being affected. She wanted to quit a job that she loved and at which she excelled, and to leave a boss she actually wanted to see succeed. From Juanita's perspective, Monique was harassing her, and she wanted to file a complaint.

Monique wasn't having it any easier. Despite concerns with Juanita's ability to contain sensitive information, Monique recognized that Juanita was her top performer, Ms. Reliable. At the same time, Monique was also hearing about Juanita's indirect complaints and frustrations. Monique couldn't figure out Juanita's frustrations because she told Juanita several times the promotion was imminent. Monique tried to give Juanita every opportunity she could. Despite that, Monique was hearing from the floor that Juanita was undermining her.

She bottled that up – what else could she do? She couldn't go out on the floor and badmouth her Team Leader. She began to keep her door closed to avoid everything, especially Juanita. More people would drop in and give her information (from slanted perspectives) about Juanita. Monique was convinced that Juanita was trying to get rid of her. She wanted to quit. The stress was unbearable.

When both were about to file harassment complaints against each other, their boss got wind of the trouble and suggested to both Juanita and Monique that they engage in a day-long, facilitated collaborative process to work out their issues with each other. Using the collaborative model, Juanita and Monique exchanged how each had impacted the other negatively by their actions and inactions. They discovered that many of those impacts were unintended or even contrary to their positive intentions. They recognized that they were interpreting everything in its worst possible light. (An expression I often use is, *when there is tension, people hear what they fear they were going to hear.*) They realized that what each wanted and wanted to avoid in their working relationship was similar. They began to understand how others fed the rumour mill and that their tuning into those rumours harmed their relationship. They generated ideas for how they could interact in a way that would strengthen their effectiveness and their relationship. They developed a way forward where they could both succeed.

From the outside, that dramatic change in a relationship might seem impossible, or at least highly improbable. That transformation would have been impossible had they continued in the adjudicative model where each perceived the other as the harasser and themselves as the victim. There's a strong likelihood that their relationship would've deteriorated and that the whole office would've been divided with them. The use of a collaborative communication model enabled them to move forward together. Note that they could've used that collaborative process at any time in their relationship, and not only when it seemed like there was no other choice available.

For Problem-Solving – Ted and Stella

Far too often in typical problem-solving, there seems to be only a couple of options and it's easy to get sucked into a process to choose between them. A collaborative process is designed to identify interests first and then options, and that order can produce totally unexpected solutions.

Bill Diepeveen, a well-known mediator in Alberta, Canada, told me this story about two neighbours and a dog that demonstrates the power of collaborative problem-solving. Ted worked night shifts and would try to sleep in the mornings. Stella next door caught her bus at 7:15 a.m., about the time that Ted was getting home. She put her dog Jasper in the outdoor kennel each day and when nearby children were passing, Jasper wanted to play. So, at the same time when Ted was trying to sleep, Stella would be gone to work and Jasper would be barking for attention from the school children. Ted called the municipality complaining under the dog bylaw, which would typically provide two options: silence the dog or get rid of it (definitely an adjudicative model).

Bill brought Ted and Stella together to see if they could find a solution using a collaborative process. Initial conversations and problem-solving generated an option which both could live with. Stella would drop Jasper off with another neighbour, who would then put the dog in the kennel well after the children were in school. This was inconvenient for Stella, yet she would do it to keep Jasper because it protected her two key interests: Jasper provided companionship and a sense of safety. She would be able to keep her dog, and Ted would get his sleep.

Stella already felt guilty enough about not being able to walk Jasper as often as she wanted to; she couldn't bear to lose him. It turned out Ted also liked dogs, and as much as the barking irritated him, he was more irritated that the dog had to spend the day locked up in the kennel. What they both really wanted to avoid was Jasper being locked up without exercise. To meet that interest, a better option was generated. Ted would walk Stella's dog, which helped him with his sleep, helped Stella with her guilt about not getting Jasper enough exercise, and strengthened their relationship as neighbours.

That solution is not one that would or could ever arise in an adjudicative model. Using a collaborative process enabled them to go beyond the surface issue, beyond a simplified compliance compromise to a more creative solution that satisfied everyone – even Jasper!

For Analysis and Decision-Making – The Community Complex

"Decision-taken" analysis in an adjudicative model is quite different from decision-making analysis in a collaborative process. The following is what happened during the construction of a community sport complex in the suburbs of a city in Canada. This community wanted its own sport complex, and a group of volunteers came together to make it happen. The group was forward-looking. They built consensus about what the complex would contain, studied other projects, raised funds, and they engaged architectural and engineering expertise. They worked as a committee where the decisions were made by motion, debate, and vote. The decisions were then recorded in minutes. Some members of the group were primarily interested in an ice rink for hockey, while others were interested in the capacity to later add an ice shed for curling. Still others saw the complex as valuable meeting and event hosting space. A few saw the opportunity to provide an exercise facility for the community. The design they approved had all components covered. Sounds collaborative, doesn't it?

All went well until, of course, the budget was getting tight on the community contribution of $800,000 to a $2.5 million project. To be within budget, they needed to shave $80,000 off the cost. The exercise facility was designed to be 40 x 80 feet. If they reduced the depth of the exercise facility on the ground floor by 10 feet, which would also reduce the professional space upstairs, they could reduce the cost and be within budget. The downside was that the change would be irreversible without significant costs.

Those whose primary concern was the ice surface presented the issue at the committee meeting. Do we go over budget or do we reduce the size so that everyone gets a bit less, but everyone gets a facility and we stay within budget? Someone moved and another seconded the motion that the design be reduced by 10 feet, as proposed.

A lengthy debate followed. No other options were considered, simply A or B. The motion carried.

The community ended up with a facility where the exercise area for its population was not suitable. It became a daycare, which was not a waste, and not what was intended, either. The professional space was abandoned because it, too, was undersized. The late design change also created leak issues, which required further repairs. There was no going back because the costs of a retrofit would outstrip $300,000. The Committee disbanded. Some members still harbour resentment to others and believe that trickery and deceit were used to sway the vote. Sound familiar?

You can see the adjudicative model at work:

1. Define the issue slanting it to the preferred outcome.
2. Present two options.
3. List the pros and cons.
4. Choose or rationalize the preferred outcome.

In an adjudicative model, the idea is to narrow options and force the preferred decision, not to expand ideas – because within the two options already being debated, one is obviously the CORRECT decision. In this case, the adjudicative model produced the ratification of the decision taken in the majority's collective mind, which was exactly the result it's designed to produce.

Were other options available? Of course, there were.

Collaborative decision-making by this committee would have looked vastly different. Even if they skipped the first step, *Set Parameters*, an exchange of perspectives would've informed participants of a broader array of viewpoints. In a collaborative model, the issue would have been framed openly, rather than as a dichotomy, as A or B. Perhaps the issue might've been framed as "what to do about the budget shortfall?" or, "how to accomplish the best outcome for the community?" or, "how to balance fiscal responsibility and community needs?" Underlying interests were probably expressed in the guise of pros and cons, and went unheard by others because participants in a debate are pre-conditioned to *listen to respond* instead of to *listen to learn.* Where interests were expressed, they weren't used to generate options, but as a choice between only two options. Lastly, when one option was chosen, no further consequential questions were asked. Those questions were presented as rhetorical questions as part of the argument during the debate of pros and cons.

The situations of Juanita and Monique, Ted and Stella, and the Community Complex, are common in everyday life. As you read, were you reminded of similar situations that you – or people you know – have experienced? For communication in working relationships, for problem-solving in everyday life in neighbourhoods, and for analysis and decision-making in organizations, the use of a collaborative process offers huge advantages and provides dramatically better outcomes than the adjudicative model produces.

If we want those enhanced outcomes, then we need to choose to be collaborative.

Collaboration – The Choice That Isn't a Choice

The shift of focus from conflict to collaboration is essential to keep pace with the evolution of the workplace. The traditional workplace was all about production, the quantity and quality of widgets. The management style used to drive production was command and control. It's certainly true that the traditional workplace continues to exist and production will always be important. It's equally true that management will probably always have some command and control features. The evolving workplace is more about a knowledge-based economy relying upon analysis, innovation, and judgment. For the new reality, we need to create supportive, engaging workplaces as an operating environment where production requires analysis, innovation and judgment. Perpetuating the adjudicative model isn't making the grade.

Leveraging diversity is important because our world is becoming increasingly complex. Perspectives with greater diversity and divergence are fuelled by the growth and availability of the information base on most subjects. That information base increasingly contains cross-linkages and implications among issues. As the information base of society increases, so do areas of specialization. The interdependence of specialists is evident in many areas, notably:

- Health – look at the increasing number of inter-disciplinary clinics.
- Business expertise – look at the expansion of firms offering accounting, marketing and legal advice under one umbrella.
- Design – the co-existence of engineering, architectural design, and construction departments.

The coordination and cooperation of specialists is essential for projects to succeed. Consequently, optimal decisions can be reached only when that diversity of perspectives and expertise is leveraged as part of the decision-making process. Using an adjudicative model as the basis for the communication, problem-solving and analysis is increasingly inadequate in our increasingly specialized world.

We must make the choice to be collaborative.

CHAPTER TWELVE

Resources and Research Consistent with Collaboration

A culture of collaboration would be supported by educating people, providing information and evidence about how humans interact and how they build and destroy relationships. In today's culture, it may be that the judgmental spirit that is essential to an adjudicative model simply renders information about how humans are wired useless? We're conditioned to analyze situations, form hypotheses/assumptions, and make decisions, essentially to apply the adjudicative model to human interactions and relationships as well as to problem-solving.

Five Universal Core Concerns

A spirit of curiosity is a prerequisite to collaboration. Curiosity would lead us to information about how humans are wired. Two resources well worth a read about our basic wiring are books by Roger Fisher and Vern Redekop. In *Beyond Reason*,[37] Fisher writes about five universal core concerns:

1. Appreciation: the need to be understood by others (especially if they disagree with us)
2. Autonomy: the need for influence over decisions affecting us
3. Affiliation: the need to feel connected
4. Role: the need to find meaning in our work
5. Status: to be respected for our knowledge of self, and for the skills we have by reason of our education, training, and experience

---

37   Roger Fisher, *Beyond Reason: Using Emotions as you Negotiate* (New York: Penguin Books, 2006).

Fisher makes the point that addressing the core concerns of others is not about gaining positive points; the value lies in avoiding negative energy. He says it's like air. If we have plenty, more doesn't matter; if we're drowning, absence of air will cause us to discharge lots of negative energy.

In *From Violence to Blessing*,[38] Redekop writes about five human identity needs, which, when not satisfied, trigger negative emotions:

1. Meaning/Justice: Anger (aligns closely with role)
2. Action: Depression (aligns with autonomy)
3. Recognition: Self-doubt/shame (status)
4. Security: Fear
5. Connectedness: Sadness (affiliation)

These human identity needs and universal core concerns align fairly closely. I prefer Fisher's approach because tying a specific emotional response to a particular need is a stretch, and I can envision situations where similar emotions could be triggered by several of those needs. I especially like how Redekop expresses that when all of our needs are met, we feel whole. These elements of humanity run deeper than interests. Whereas interests are often compatible, these elements are more universally shared. In a culture of collaboration, at least at a basic level these concepts would be broadly understood.

The Internal Critic

In *Difficult Conversations*,[39] Douglas Stone and his colleagues write about how conversations become difficult because they impact our sense of identity. It is as if we have an internal critic that continually assesses our actions against three criteria:

- Competence
- Ethics

---

38   Vern Neufeld Redekop, *From Violence to Blessing: How an Understanding of Deep-Rooted Conflict Can Open Paths to Reconciliation* (Ottawa: Novalis Publications, 2002).

39   Douglas Stone, Bruce Patton, and Sheila Heen, *Difficult Conversations: How to Discuss What Matters Most* (New York: Penguin Books, 1999) 111-116.

- Worthiness of Love

That internal critic is also continually assessing the impact of our behaviours upon the perceptions of others – do others think we are:

- Competent?
- Ethical?
- Worthy of love?

This internal critic encourages our avoidance of difficult conversations for fear of triggering a negative assessment. When we get a negative assessment, we generate negative energy like we do when those five universal core concerns are not addressed. It's often the case that negative energy, fear, and defensiveness are related to the volume at which our internal critic screams out its assessment. In this way, the three criteria serve as tools to help figure out both ourselves and others. Remember earlier, when you read that piece about electronic communications? It is this internal critic that interprets the electronic message, regardless of what words are used in accordance with my maxim: "People hear what they fear they were going to hear."

Other important evidence can be found in the research of the Gallup organization and its publication *First, Break All the Rules*.[40] The Gallup organization's research demonstrates that when people join a workplace, they want three key things:

- To belong
- To contribute
- To grow together

These three aspirations also act like Fisher's five universal core concerns. They align closely with Affiliation, Role, and Status. If people are expressing strong negative energy in your workplace, is that expression related to one of those needs not being addressed?

---

40   Marcus Buckingham and Curtis Coffman, *First, Break All the Rules: What The World's Greatest Managers Do Differently* (New York: Simon and Schuster, 1999) 39-43. This research product from the Gallup Organization explains how organizations identify, attract, and retain, talented employees. This research is based on over a million employees and 80,000 managers.

While the Gallup organization was studying paid workplaces, I don't see any reason why their research results would not apply to any other workplace as I defined it earlier.

The Gottmans' "Love Lab"

Turning to another evidence base, the research and findings from the Gottman Institute[41] about relationships would be broadly understood within a culture of collaboration. Since a stronger relationship is one of the two outcomes deliberately pursued in collaboration, evidence about how relationships work is important. In today's culture, the formation and deterioration of relationships seems haphazard and not well understood at all. The Gottman research provides a conceptualization of relationships that is transferable to the workplace. While the Gottmans studied marriage, many people also have a "work spouse." The principles and patterns conducive to healthy spousal relationships are therefore equally applicable to healthy work spouse relationships, and relationships with other colleagues at all levels. The basics and beyond are well explained in *The Relationship Cure*.[42]

The Gottmans were searching for the secret to successful marriages and the cause of failed ones. In their love lab, couples were metered for blood pressure, pulse, breath rate, body temperature, even sensors for fidgeting in the seat when conversations got dicey! Their interactions were video-taped and observed by a team of psychologists through one-way glass. Their research extended over more than 30

41 "Love Lab," The Gottman Institute (2019), accessed July 31, 2019, https://www.gottman.com/love-lab/. This site provides an interesting summary and background. Dr. John Gottman began to study relationships in couples in the 1970s, and since then, more than three thousand couples have been observed in his "love lab." In 1996, Drs. Julie and John Gottman co-founded the Gottman Institute. The evidence and principles derived from their research remain applicable to any relationship. Gottman's conceptualization of effective and ineffective patterns in communication and relationships is extremely useful and his research provides a strong evidentiary basis for the effectiveness of the collaborative communication model presented in this book.

42 John Gottman and Joan DeClaire, *The Relationship Cure: a 5 Step Guide to Strengthening Your Marriage, Family, and Friendships* (New York: Three Rivers Press, 2001) 4.

years. That level of effort could well be expected to produce reliable evidence about how relationships work.

The Gottmans' observations of relationships flesh out Stephen Covey's idea of the emotional bank account.[43] What they observed was that relationships are built (emotional bank accounts are operated) through a series of "emotional bids" (Gottman and DeClaire, 2001, 8) and responses. An emotional bid is anything that indicates a sense of or desire for connection with another person, anything from a smile to a deep conversation. Each emotional bid and appropriate response is a deposit into that emotional bank account that we keep with each other. This research provides evidence that a healthy relationship has at least a 5:1 ratio of deposits to withdrawals (ibid., 5). As Gottman conceptualizes communication and relationships, the emotional bid is the basic unit and the bid and response pattern is how relationships are built and how they are maintained. Gottman says that emotional intelligence is the capacity to bid and respond appropriately (ibid., 24).

The bid pattern is like a tennis warm up: you volley, the other returns; you return, they return. Well, maybe you do . . . or maybe you don't. Does it matter, for example, when someone says good morning to you and you do not respond? Or how you respond? Gottman says you have three choices in how you respond to an emotional bid (ibid.,16):

- Turn toward
- Turn away
- Turn against

Okay, so you have three choices, and on any day or with any individual bid, you may choose any of them. Does your choice matter?

I was surprised at this statistic from their research. Are you?

---

43   Stephen R. Covey, *The 7 Habits of Highly Effective People: Restoring the Character Ethic* (New York: Free Press, 2004) 188. Covey suggests we each keep an emotional bank account with those near us. If we constantly withdraw from our emotional bank account, it has the same impact as withdrawing continually from a monetary bank account.

> Even in a healthy relationship, when there is no posi-
> tive response to the bid, there is an ***80 percent*** chance
> that the bidder will not bid again [in any reasonable
> future time] (ibid., 18).

A full 80 percent in a healthy spousal relationship! What do you
think happens in a tense relationship? What does that say about
the importance of everyday niceties, what people call small talk, in
our workplace?

Gottman and his team kept watching for the formation of deeply-
connected marriages. How were those formed and nurtured? They
concluded that these successful marriages were not based upon
moments of deep connection. Instead, the evidence showed that the
basis was the bid exchange about things like "how was your day?"
"I'm getting a cup of tea – would you like one?"

According to this research, there are six main reasons why the
bid exchange breaks down. Gottman's six bid busters (Gottman and
DeClaire, 2001, 50-51) are:

- Inattention/preoccupation
- Sour Note Start-up
- Criticism
- Flooding
- Negativity
- Avoidance

According to the Gottman research, 96 percent of the time, the
first three minutes of a conversation predicts its outcome (ibid., 69).
A criticism breaks the bid exchange because it usually triggers a defensive response. "Flooding" (ibid., 72) is the word Gottman uses to
describe that state of being emotionally and physically overwhelmed
where we cannot engage in an exchange. This has to do with the
limbic portion of our brain becoming flooded when it perceives a
threat. The more advanced pre-frontal cortex's ability to address the
situation/stimuli and provide a socially appropriate response becomes
disabled. Negativity is a bid-buster because it simply wears people
down. Avoidance in its most negative context leads to an eventual

attack. The attack is often in the form of the *Blurt* conversation that I mentioned earlier.

Gottman's research identifies three universal emotional needs (ibid., 19):

- To be included
- To have a sense of control
- To be liked

This should be no great surprise given what was said above about universal core concerns and human identity needs. On the opposite side of the coin are four behaviours that are destined to destroy relationships. Gottman calls them the "Four Horsemen of the Apocalypse" (ibid., 51) in relationships:

- Criticism
- Defensiveness
- Stonewalling
- Contempt

A relationship that exhibits these behaviours has a very poor chance of survival.

Gottman's evidence about healthy relationships, how people communicate, how they form relationships – these ideas would be broadly known and understood within a culture of collaboration. In our existing culture of adjudication, I would guess that a very small portion of the population is even aware of the Gottman research, though, and of that portion, a minuscule number would use it.

It's seldom that group dynamic issues do not revolve around communication and relationships. As groups start to spiral downwards, avoidance adds momentum. A local entrepreneur who worked with me in community groups has this expression about businesses: "It's far easier to make a good business great, than a bad business good." That same principle applies to relationships.

In a culture of collaboration, it will be important to work from frameworks with an evidentiary basis that enables us to strengthen communication, relationships, analysis and problem-solving. These sources of evidence exist; we just are not using them.

CHAPTER THIRTEEN

Direct Benefits from Integrating the Collaborative Model

Four specific activities would be positively impacted by integrating the collaborative model:

- Innovation
- Analysis
- Community group decision-making
- Strategic planning

Innovation

I can see where especially younger readers might think: "A new collaborative model for problem-solving? No thanks, we already have a better way!"

Those readers may be thinking that they don't need this collaborative model because they have the latest and greatest or the most time-tested and true model for problem-solving. They are into LEAN, Agile, Six Sigma, the Toyota Eight Step, and other recent innovation models.

Here's where it gets tricky. Each of these innovation process models requires conversations to support problem-solving. Without integrating the collaborative model, these processes will struggle with the *Bottle,* the *Blurt,* and the *Blab* because they still depend on conversations and relationships in order to be effective.

Remember that this collaborative model is a universal problem-solving process for the workplace. The processes that I've identified above are intended to expedite innovation. While some may use elements of the collaborative model already, each of these innovation models can be enhanced by embedding the collaborative model within it. Aligning the collaborative model with any of the above isn't a stretch, and alignment is important to enhance conversations to support problem-solving. It's generally accepted that change, communication, and conflict are inseparable. Continual improvement, communication, and collaboration are equally inseparable. Communicating collaboratively gives us our best chance to make change that results in continual improvement.

Equally, this new collaborative model can be embedded within ancient traditional problem-solving models. For example, when I was working in eastern Canada with a First Nations group accustomed to using a community Circle process, they told me their traditional process lacked the element of follow through. By incorporating a collaborative process within their traditional Circle, they addressed the weakness they perceived in their communal approach to situations. The reality testing in the *Select Solutions* step focuses on details around who will do what, and when. That final focus on details provided them with a mechanism to strengthen their follow through.

As a second example, while I was working in western Canada with a group using a peace building circle as the format for a restorative process, we incorporated a collaborative approach to improve the action planning that the group needed in order to move forward. This new collaborative model is so universal that it is easily adapted and embedded within any group problem-solving process. What this six-step collaborative model adds to any problem-solving process is **logic to strengthen outcomes**. What this collaborative model brings to relationships is **reduction of tension to strengthen relationships**.

Within the federal government in Canada, an organization called the National Managers Community (NMC) developed a series of leadership and learning tools in an effort to effect change. Listening to the stories of those who used them, it was apparent that the largest obstacle to effectiveness was that facilitators didn't have a process step or tool to start things off on a solid footing when there was tension present within a group. To bridge that gap, I developed an additional tool, "Parameters for Participation," which mirrors step one of the collaborative model, *Set Parameters*. In a culture of collaboration, these tools (or ones similar to them) could be broadly used by any facilitator familiar with the collaborative model. Their use would strengthen problem-solving within workplaces.

Two NMC tools I particularly like are the "Interview Matrix" and the "Feedback Model" both of which are easy to use and effective. The Interview Matrix is like speed dating, and it enables the input of a group to be gathered around a series of four key issues, concerns or challenges the group wants to address. This tool can gather input very quickly, accommodate styles of introversion and extraversion easily, and enable a group to reach a broad-based consensus in a short period of time.

Feedback is absolutely essential to enable people to contribute and to grow together in any workplace. In our judgmental culture using the adjudicative model, feedback has a negative connotation such that people seldom seek it and people often fear it. In a culture of collaboration, feedback would be sought eagerly and offered generously as a normal part of interaction.

The NMC model anticipates that the person receiving feedback has their own ideas about how they performed. The model therefore enables the receiver to offer their self-assessment to create space to receive feedback from someone else. What makes the model simple is that it's based on using the same three questions:

- What do you think went well?
- What was tricky?
- What would you do differently next time?

So, the model starts with the observer asking the performer these three questions. When the performer has provided their responses, then the observer provides their thoughts on those same three questions. The model provides a balance of strengths and weaknesses with a focus on the future or growth opportunity. While the exchange may or may not open a dialogue, the performer's simple response of "thank you" is sufficient to close the feedback process. This expression of gratitude is an acknowledgement that feedback is a gift that others give us with the positive intent to help us learn and improve continually.

The Importance of Diverse Thinking

Innovation and problem-solving depend necessarily upon diversity of thought. That interdependence exists almost by definition, because if diverse thinking wasn't required, then it wouldn't really be a problem of any significance in the first place. In the diversity conversation, it's the area of thought that is most often overlooked. While it's true that people can make judgments of others based on race, creed, gender, or some other unjustified basis, we judge each other's thoughts and ideas more frequently than anything else about them. A conference speaker once stated that in the diversity conversation, diversity of thought is the orphan.

The impact of early judgment of ideas is immense. In a typical meeting or forum, only a small number of people speak. Are those who speak the extroverts and those remaining silent all introverts? Does that really make any sense? In your next experience of that scenario, throw out this hypothesis and watch:

> *I have noticed that only a few have voiced your ideas; I am guessing that those who have not spoken have ideas, and that the reason you have not spoken is that you do not want to open your thoughts to being judged by others. How many of you does that resonate with?*

When I have tested that idea, many of the silent majority were nodding their heads. That fear of being judged is directly attributable to our adoption of the adjudicative model as the norm.

In a culture of collaboration, diversity of thought would be encouraged and valued. The things most dramatically different in a culture of collaboration would be:

- An approach based on curiosity that values diversity of thought from the outset
- Processes and tools to harness diverse perspectives
- The identification of interests before the generation of options

How groups get there can vary. Having this collaborative model as a logical process guide enables facilitators to use a variety of tools and techniques to adapt to situations and scenarios, working toward the ultimate objective of enabling the group to arrive at collaborative outcomes. That may simply mean understanding the perspective and underlying interests of those with whom we disagree, and yes, even an agreement to disagree respectfully.

Analysis

Written analysis supports many workplaces from government to private sector business to non-profit community organizations – pretty well every element of a knowledge-based economy. As I said earlier, sound decision-making depends on analysis. In each of those settings, the template may vary in name and format. That said, by whatever labels, written analysis generally will have these components:

- Problem/Issue
- Facts/Context/Background
- Options
- Considerations/Discussion/Pros and Cons
- Recommended Option/Proposal/Next Steps

The format is inherently adjudicative. Those relying on these products value three writing qualities, which are often referred to as persuasive or strategic writing skills. These three are:

- Concision
- Clarity
- Brevity

Shouldn't the reader of an analysis of any issue reasonably expect it to have those qualities?

Analysis using the collaborative model would look quite different than what I described above. Analysis using the collaborative model would have those same qualities except applied to a different series of components. The components of a collaborative analysis paper would be:

- Presenting Issues
- Informing Perspectives

- Key Interests to be Satisfied in a Solution
- Options to Satisfy Interests
- Alignment of Options with Interests
- Proposed Solution (including Reality-Testing Considerations)

The discussion about how well the options aligned with key interests would be the heart of the analysis. While both products should be well written, the collaborative one will have higher strategic value.

In the collaborative model, it's the logic within the model that enables the product to be described as strategic and analytical. It is strategic to the extent that it aligns with and furthers the vision that the workplace or organization seeks to implement; it is analytical to the extent that it identifies the key interests, options to satisfy those, and assesses the options against those interests as the criteria for selecting the best options.

Obviously, and sadly, most citizens don't have to look far to see examples of poor decisions in their community organizations, or by their local or national governing institutions – decisions lacking collaborative-based analysis.

Community Decision-Making

Perhaps the group with the most to gain is that volunteer committee operating on a debate-and-vote model of analysis and decision-making. Meetings using a collaborative model would look quite different from the traditional style. Issues would be framed openly, and open for reframing if participants found the initial statement to be too restrictive. The perspectives of each participant would be heard. Chairs of meetings would have a stronger inclination to facilitation. The six steps of the model would be embedded in the flow of the meeting, and participants would assist each other to identify the interests that were embedded in their perspectives. Those interests, once identified, would be the focus of generating ideas for moving forward, and they would be reflected in a solid solution. That solution or decision would then be recorded via the motion and vote process. Talent would leave those committees when the work they wanted to complete was done, or when the subject matter no longer held their interest – not because they didn't feel heard.

Group Planning Exercises

Planning exercises for groups (and teams) would also be strengthened in a culture of collaboration. The standard tools reflect some variation of the "strengths, weaknesses, opportunities, threats" (SWOT) tool. The traditional SWOT tool would benefit by incorporating collaborative exercises and tools designed to harness diverse perspectives. The whole process would be marked with a "listen to learn" versus a "listen to respond" dynamic.

A common complaint about planning exercises is that they produce ideas that have no chance or hope of being implemented. So, a beautiful report gets compiled of ideas that were developed with the voice of the few and never subjected to any reality or feasibility testing. The report sits on the shelf because no critical mass within the organization is invested in it and its content is of questionable value. Incorporating a collaborative process within the planning session would strengthen commitment, improve ideas, and strengthen relationships among the planning participants.

CHAPTER FOURTEEN

Building the Culture – Individual, Group/Team, and Institutional

A culture is the product of the choices that individuals comprising the group make in their everyday business of life. As more individuals embrace this collaborative model, a culture of collaboration will grow. In order to accelerate that growth, effort, and choices can be made at three levels: the individual, the group, and the institution.

As you read this, are you wondering how you can influence your workplace to move toward a culture of collaboration – what can you do? Can you make a difference by yourself? History is filled with stories of individuals who have made a difference. Sometimes, to illustrate that point, analogies are used like that of the mosquito in a tent. As well, there is the story of the small boy walking along the beach, picking up starfish that had washed ashore, and throwing them back in. He was only one boy, and the starfish were plastered all over the beach. A man was curious about the boy's efforts and asked what he was doing. The boy responded that he was saving the starfish. The man laughed and said, "There are millions of starfish on the shore and you are only one small boy. How could you possibly make a difference?" The boy bent over, picked up one of the millions of starfish and he tossed it back into the water. He looked at the man and said, "I made a difference to that one!"

The point of these stories is that every significant change has begun with one individual in circumstances where it otherwise would've seemed impossible to make a difference.

Choose to Communicate Collaboratively – Three Skills for the Big Three

The most effective thing that any individual can do to create a culture of collaboration is to choose to communicate collaboratively. It is within the power of each individual to have the Big Three conversations in a collaborative manner. I suggested earlier that these three conversations significantly impact the health of every workplace and can happen using a collaborative communication model.

I say this with confidence because I've taught people to do just that. This six-step collaborative model can be incorporated into a five-minute conversation. Interestingly, this does not depend on both participants comprehending the collaborative model. As long as one person in the conversation understands the model, it will typically work out successfully.

Recall that on page 22, I described an evaluation of whether workshop participants used the collaborative skills from the workshop and whether the impact was positive or negative. The results from those evaluations indicated that more than 80 percent of participants used the communication skills with a significantly positive impact. Now, I'm going to focus on how to incorporate this collaborative model within an ordinary complaint. Note that Gottman distinguishes between a complaint and a criticism (ibid., 72). A criticism is exemplified by a conversation in which the speaker describes the event or behaviour that isn't working for them AND ascribes the responsibility for that negative impact entirely to the other person: "You are at fault when this happens!"

A complaint is the description of an event or behaviour that is not working for the speaker, where the speaker requests change without indicating in any way that the listener is at fault or to blame. Gottman says that complaints are a good thing (ibid., 72). Were it not for complaints, we might not have shelter, nor agriculture, nor water wells. At some point, someone complained that caves were dark and scary, or that they desired a consistent food supply instead of having to forage randomly. The same might be said of fresh water supplies. Indeed, the same may be said of any innovation, convenience, or what we now consider necessities. The collaborative communication workshop I developed in 2011 is about equipping people to complain effectively.

"C-Message" to Address the "Bottle"

So, how do we change the conversation from the *Bottle*, the *Blurt*, and the *Blab* using a collaborative model? We do so by simplifying the conversation so that it mirrors the collaborative model. So, for the *Bottle* in a collaborative model, we can use a "collaborative message" (or "**c-message**") to complain effectively.

Some readers may have had training in some form of assertiveness communication. That type of training has a variety of points of emphasis, such as:

- make clear requests
- express your emotions
- focus on your impact
- use "I" rather than "you" statements
- express how it made you feel

While all of these have positive aspects, none are really collaborative. When I deliver workshops on using this collaborative model for communication, I show participants how they can change the *Bottle* conversation in their head to a collaborative conversation with the other person using a **c-message** that mirrors this six-step collaborative model. A well-constructed c-message has five components that each reflect an element of the collaborative model. They are:

- Describing the event or behaviour being complained about in non-judgmental language.
- Describing your experience as an impact or an emotion (either works).
- Relating the impact to your underlying interest.
- Offering an option or showing openness to options.
- Inviting the other person to engage in problem-solving with you.

Remember how the *Set Parameters* step is intended to create a safe environment so as to minimize defensive responses? The use of non-judgmental language in the first component has that same effect: it signals to the listener that they are not being attacked, hence no need for defensiveness.

The second component of this c-message is the sharing of the speaker's perspective without attribution of fault or blame. The absence of fault enables the listener to hear the speaker's perspective, and it creates an appreciation of how the speaker has been impacted. This component mirrors the *Exchange Perspectives* step of the collaborative model.

In the third component, the speaker relates the impact to their unmet interest, mirroring the *Identify Interests* step of the collaborative model. In most training designed to enable participants to make effective requests (like non-violent communication or assertiveness training), this step of relating impact to unmet interest is omitted. Skipping this step is like skipping *Identify Interests* in the collaborative model. When this step is skipped, the "option" presented in the next step usually comes across as an ultimatum.

In a c-message, the speaker offers a suggestion for future situations, or alternatively, a desire to develop or entertain ideas from the listener. That option is presented as totally open for discussion. This exploratory quality mimics the *Generate Options* step of this collaborative model where an idea is offered as a potential way to address the problem in order to address the interest identified. Similarly, the future option is presented without explanation or defence or rationalization.

Lastly, in a c-message, the speaker invites the listener to engage in the problem-solving, using what are often said to be the four most important words in human relations: "what do you think?"[44] In an adjudicative model of communication, there's no need for any engagement of the other person beyond their concession to your request, which again, lands like an ultimatum.

Moving from conceptualization to implementation, what words does one use? In order to support transitioning to collaborative communication, I created a template for the c-message. When my

---

44   The importance attached to these four words is a reference to the works of Elton Mayo in the 1920s and 30s. Mayo is considered to be the father of Human Relations Theory.

participants practiced with this template, they said that it felt awkward on first try, and that with even a second opportunity to practice, their comfort increased.

The most difficult portion of the c-message is finding the neutral language, especially when you are feeling the tension in the situation you want to address. Two tendencies exist when people try to use the c-message:

1. They end up dancing around the issue, such that the listener becomes confused and has no idea what the issue is.
2. They use language that is judgemental, such that the listener becomes defensive.

How to deal with these? For the first one, if you avoid a preamble, you will avoid the dance. An effective c-message will be only five short sentences. To avoid using judgmental language, I recommend quiet reflection to find the balance between sugar-coating what you want to say and blaming the other person.

Now of course, there's no crystal ball, and people do not come with software and manuals. So, you can never be sure. That uncertainty doesn't mean you should avoid the conversation though. In a culture of collaboration, people become accustomed to communicating collaboratively – in the same manner as they do after my workshops. By using the c-message on a widespread basis as the norm, the *Bottle* conversation and avoidance decrease dramatically.

When this book is complete, I'll be working on a toolbox for collaboration. Within it, you will find tools and templates to strengthen your capacity for collaboration, including my c-message template.

De-escalation and Re-orientation to Address the "Blurt"

Widespread use of c-messages will not eliminate all avoidance, and therefore some *Blurt* conversations will happen. Addressing the *Blurt* involves a process of **de-escalation and re-orientation**. As a short form, I refer to it as the "D&R skill." The D&R skill is more difficult to use than the c-message. Firstly, the responder is caught by surprise and has no preparation time. Secondly, the language used in the *Blurt* is accusatory and judgmental, and a natural initial defensiveness arises. So, let's look at each component of this skill separately.

De-escalation is a process whereby the responder explores the *Blurt* in such a way that the Blurter senses acknowledgement, which defuses the emotional charge. Re-orientation is a communication process whereby the responder decodes the underlying interest of the Blurter and reframes the *Blurt* in such a way that both can approach it as if it had been spoken in the c-message format. While that sounds complicated, it really isn't.

The key is to remember that the *Blurt* is not about the responder, it's about the unmet needs of the Blurter. Think about it this way: if all of your interests as I've described them above were being satisfied, then you would be a happy camper, right? You become negatively charged when these aren't being addressed. If you release that charge at me, your energy is about your unmet needs, not my actions. So, the first thing to remember in a *Blurt* conversation is that it's not all about you. Put another way, as a colleague often says, "just because one person is uncomfortable doesn't mean that the other did something wrong."

De-escalating works because of the power of listening, and it goes deeper than that. More accurately, the act of listening can be performed with different levels of impact. Almost everyone has heard of the importance of listening, and yet few understand why it's important. Many people glaze over when they hear someone speak about the importance of listening. It's worth a few paragraphs to position the act of listening within the context of how human beings are wired, in an effort to remove that glaze.

I've mentioned above the five universal core concerns noted by Fisher: Appreciation, Autonomy, Affiliation, Role, and Status. (I've also mentioned the human identity needs about which Redekop wrote.) Now, let's look at the power of listening within the context of those concerns and needs. The simple act of passive listening (in silence) is a minimal yet surprisingly effective way to respond to that need for connection that these authors describe. Listening has power and value because it demonstrates Affiliation.

In the de-escalation, the listening goes beyond passivity. The skill user acknowledges the impact being expressed by the Blurter. That acknowledgement itself responds to the Blurter's core concerns for Appreciation and Status. Accordingly, the Blurter feels acknowledged, which is the last thing they ever expected – that's why they did the *Blurt* in the first place!

Watch what happens though, if the responder instead reaches for their innocent intent and gives that explanation *before* acknowledging impact. In that case, what the Blurter hears is that the responder is not listening, does not care about the impact they have had, and that they are interested only in excusing themselves. Until there is acknowledgement of impact, the explanation of innocent intent is wasted words. Reversing the order adds insult to injury from the Blurter's perspective. That effect seems obvious and makes sense in the context of Fisher and Redekop's texts about how we are wired.

If the source of the *Blurt* is an unmet interest, then the key to de-escalation is identifying that interest. I had said above that the key attitude to collaboration is curiosity. In de-escalation, the responder is remembering that the *Blurt* is not about them, and exercises curiosity to figure out what is the unmet interest. While the responder may be tempted to ask "why," that word by itself often triggers a defensive and escalating reaction. So, in a collaborative model of communication, the responder goes about exercising curiosity without asking any why questions.

I encourage the use of a series of questions that I refer to as "Curiosity Queries"[45] to assist the responder. These questions obtain information without using the word "why." Once the responder has a theory about the Blurter's unmet interest, they express their hunch. This is often in the form of an "it sounds like X is important to you . . ." statement. The Blurter experiences this hunch as an effort to address their core concerns for Appreciation, Affiliation and Status.

---

45   This is one of the tools that will be included *in The Collaborator's Toolbox*, my upcoming book. Stay tuned!

While it's difficult to describe, it's easy to notice in practice when the responder has identified the unmet interest of the Blurter. The affirmation is clear in the Blurter's response, and a significant de-escalation happens immediately. As I described earlier, the greater the level of tension, the more invisible the underlying interests are, even to the Blurter. This de-escalation relates back to those universal core concerns. When the responder identifies the Blurter's unmet interest, that identification is a sign of Appreciation, that the responder understands the experience of the Blurter. That identification also addresses the Blurter's need for Affiliation. Fisher says that when negative energy arises, address the core concern, not the energy, and that by doing so, the negative energy will dissipate (Fisher, 2006, 203). That is exactly what happens at that point. Once de-escalation has been achieved, then re-orientation can begin.

Re-orientation kicks into high gear once the unmet interest has been identified. Gordon Sloan uses a future-focused spin for this. The importance of the future-focused spin is to point the conversation away from the past. In its absence, the wounded Blurter will often cycle back to their pain, despite the acknowledgment of the responder's impact. The future-focused spin breaks that cycle.

Now, the responder is able to repackage the information they have in such a way that both participants can talk about the situation as a complaint, not a criticism. That is to say, the responder reframes the *Blurt* as if it had been presented as a c-message. With the problem repositioned as a complaint, each participant can talk about their own interests and decide how they want to go forward. At this point, the explanation of innocent intent can be heard – essentially the responder's perspective – and then they can both go to the future-focus, which is often a "what do we do now or next time?" type of question. The engagement of the Blurter, going forward in the problem-solving, responds to the concern for Autonomy: it gives the Blurter influence over what happens next.

The following is a reproduction from one of my workshops of a practice conversation using the D&R skill. The participants are Susan and Gayle, and each of them was given one of the following parts of the scenario:

> **Skill User** – Susan: You are on a small committee of five people, all very animated, trying to improve office morale. You were really hoping for people to be solution-oriented, but they keep complaining about things like workload pressures, lack of resources, having to do work that is not value-added, and mixed messages from upper management. You are a supervisor and you don't want to shut them down and you don't want them to stay focused on the negative. How long do you let this go?

> **Blurter** – Gayle: You joined this committee because you think there are things that the office can do to improve morale, no matter what management does. Sure, there is workload pressure, and yes, it would be nice to have more bodies to do the work, and there are always parts of the work that don't make a lot of sense to do. But, if the group would just focus on what it can do, that would be far more productive than moaning and groaning like they do now. You have listened to them all going on and on, and Gayle, who is chairing it, is just letting it go. You reach the end of your rope and state quite loudly, "Come on. This meeting is getting out of control. I thought we came here to make decisions, not to rant about things we can't change!"

The Conversation:

> Gayle: Come on. This meeting is getting out of control. I thought we came here to make decisions, not to rant about things we can't change!
> Susan: You seem pretty frustrated about this meeting.
> Gayle: I am totally frustrated. This negativity is killing me.
> Susan: Tell me more about what is happening for you right now?

Gayle: It's draining; we just go in circles. I think we are missing out on chances to do some positive things. This is just whining and complaining.

Susan: So, when the group goes to the negative, the impact on you is that it is like wasting your time, because making progress is important to you.

Gayle: Bingo!

Susan: Making progress and a positive impact is important to me too. Ensuring that people feel heard is, too. How do we balance giving people a chance to vent and ensuring we make progress?

Gayle: What if we set a time limit for each person?

Susan: What if we agree that for everything anyone complains about, they have to offer a solution?

Gayle: Maybe we try both for the next meeting. Maybe we need to start with "I have a solution" before saying what the problem is we want to complain about?

Susan: If I restructure the meeting format and we have an agreement on how we will proceed, I could see that working for all of us.

Gayle: Let's go with that.

As you can see in their exchange, Susan recognized that Gayle's energy was being driven by unmet needs. She explored Gayle's perspective, identified her need for making progress, which de-escalated the energy. Susan then moved to the future, re-orienting the conversation and bringing Gayle with her.

The Worry about Condescension

One concern I hear in my workshops is that using collaborative communication skills may be perceived as condescension. This concern is greatest around the *Blurt* conversation like the one reproduced above. During the de-brief from the practice exercises though, the Blurters indicate that the de-escalation was effective, and they did not sense that the skill user was being condescending at all. Interestingly, it's the observers of the practice who express that concern about condescension.

Why the difference? Their experiences are different because the skill user is interacting with the Blurter, not with the observer. In that interaction, the skill user is addressing the core concerns of the Blurter. The Blurter therefore senses Appreciation, Affiliation, and Autonomy. When the Blurter's concerns are addressed, the Blurter experiences this as caring, not condescension. In contrast, the observer is detached and experiences condescension, not caring, because the skill user is not addressing the observer's core concerns. This difference in perception again demonstrates how important those core concerns really are.

This skill is more difficult to use than the c-message, even for those who are trained in the collaborative model. When I teach this skill, I break it down into sections to make it easier. Although it's never easy, the *Blurt* conversation can be addressed using the collaborative model to de-escalate and re-orient the conversation to focus on the underlying complaint, enabling the participants to engage in effective problem-solving.

Sounding Board to Address the "Blab"

As I expressed earlier, the *Blab* is a classic conversation using the adjudicative model. When Paul blabs to his colleague Sophie about Kate, he is communicating two additional messages for which he doesn't use any words:

1. If Kate did this to me, watch out, she will do it to you.
2. If I am upset with Kate and you are my confidante, then you should be upset with her, too.

The *Blab* has been with us forever, and it's not going away. It can be drastically improved by incorporating the collaborative model within it, not by Paul the Blabber, but instead by Sophie the listener. In collaborative communication Sophie becomes an effective sounding board, whereas in the *Blab*, she was a camp-building prospect. In collaborative communication, using a **sounding board** skill, she uses an attitude of curiosity to prevent herself from becoming wrapped up in the drama. It's as if by serving as the sounding board, she shields herself from those two messages.

When Paul approaches Sophie with his *Blab*, he's discharging negative energy similar to the way he would in a *Blurt*. For Sophie, she has an easier time as the sounding board than as the responder to the *Blurt* because she's not the target of the *Blab*. Therefore, that initial defensiveness isn't triggered.

Sophie as the skill user responding to the *Blab*, asks Paul questions and paraphrases the situation and its impact on him. The sounding board skill mirrors the collaborative model. Again, the process of aiding the Blabber to identify their unmet interest is quite similar to the last skill – it's just easier to do without that initial defensiveness.

The Sounding Board Traps!

Just because the initial defensiveness is absent doesn't mean that this skill is without challenges. Four traps exist for the user of the sounding board skill, as workshops that I've delivered consistently demonstrate:

1. Wanting to agree with the *Blab*
2. Making excuses for Kate
3. Engaging in fact finding, and
4. Telling Paul what he should do

The temptation to agree with the Blabber is always strong because the Blabber usually blabs to someone whom they think and expect will agree with them. Making excuses for Kate is a technique of avoidance. Engaging in fact-finding sounds like it should be an okay activity. The problem is that once the listener becomes increasingly aware of detailed facts, they are inclined to conclude that either Paul is right, or Kate is. And, so the issue with fact-finding is that the listener becomes judgmental and entwined in the problem and ends up taking sides. When the listener tells the Blabber what they "should" do, they usurp the Blabber's right – and probably responsibility – for self-determination. Another concern is that what may work for the listener may be something that the Blabber is not able to make work. If that solution blows up, then the listener will be implicated. It's far better for the listener to adopt the mantra, "No solution is a good solution until it is their solution."

The key prerequisites to using this skill are a spirit of curiosity and a commitment to self-determination. With those as a foundation, using this skill is mainly an exercise in asking open questions until the Blabber figures out what their unmet interests are, and what they need to do about their problem in order to have their interests addressed. (Examples of open-ended questions are available in a simple internet search.)

In the same way that the listener in the *Blurt* decoded the *Blurt* and repackaged it as a c-message, the listener in the *Blab* does that same repackaging. When the Blabber can see their criticism within the *Blab* now presented back to them as a complaint in the form of a c-message, they are able to process it differently. They usually end up with a good sense of how they want to approach directly the person they were blabbing about.

In a culture of collaboration, this sounding board skill would be commonly used as a coaching process, and the *Blab* would be replaced by a request for a sounding board conversation with a peer, neighbour, or colleague.

Summary on Communicating Collaboratively

Going back to the definition of conflict as problem plus tension, we communicate to solve problems. We communicate to address tension in all of our relationships. Communicating is an activity that pervades our lives. Therefore, the first step toward creating a culture of collaboration is to embed the collaborative model within ordinary communication every day, in every workplace. Since conversations are the foundation of relationships, it would be important to replace the *Bottle*, the *Blurt,* and the *Blab* with the c-message, the de-escalation and re-orientation, and the sounding board conversations. The advantage of starting with everyday communication is that it engrains the process of collaboration across a broad base within society.

Supporting Group Use of the New Model

What if your workplace is a team or group or committee, and you're the only one who's reading this book? Can you lead the group through a collaborative problem-solving discussion? Even if you're not in a structural leadership role, and even if the group culture is well established, this is possible. One option is to offer to moderate group discussions. Another is to introduce the thought that you think the group can strengthen its capacity for collaboration and make even better decisions by using a collaborative model. As you have seen, the collaborative model can be explained in a fairly simple fashion.

For those who have introduced innovation processes like Agile or LEAN into their workplaces, the introduction of the collaborative model is no different. Assuming that the group is operating on an adjudicative model, you'll be initiating change by adopting this collaborative model. An important idea in leading change is not to be critical of the past as much as positive about the future. Envision the group as you would like to see it function. William Bridges talks about people taking a piece of the past with them[46] into the new change. One piece of the past is the opportunity to influence the best decisions possible, even when your voice might reflect a minority viewpoint. If the group is collaborating, everyone is at some time or other going to be voicing a minority perspective.

Leading the group discussion through the six steps is far easier if you don't have a desired outcome. If you serve as the moderator and you trust the logic of the process, you have to keep your eye on only one objective at each step. Your absence of a preferred outcome makes it easier for you to focus on the process. As you become more comfortable with the process, you can inject a perspective and identify your interests without dominating or steering the group. Pursue progress, not perfection. Even the most skilled facilitators make process choices they would like back – I know I have. If you make a

---

46   William Bridges, *Managing Transitions: Making the Most of Change* (Philadelphia: Perseus Books Group, 2009) 35.

mistake, stop and go back. Your colleagues will appreciate that level of transparency and authenticity.

In this section, I'm repeating some portions that you can use with your group so that you don't have to flip back to find them.

As for the first step, leading the group to establish parameters for participation is no different than I described earlier, by saying: "before we get to the merits of our views, how about we take a few minutes to talk about how we want to have a productive discussion?" It's often a good idea to provide a "pass" option with groups, with the proviso that those who pass get a chance to input when the round completes.

When each has contributed, anyone can begin the exchange of perspectives. Ask participants for their perspective by using a simple phrase like, "What is your perspective?" and to subsequent participants, "Do you have a different perspective?" It's usually easier to guide if the group proceeds either clockwise or counter-clockwise. If you use a pass option, resist the urge to reverse direction; simply carry on in one direction, giving the assurance that those who passed will get an opportunity when the question comes back around.

After each has provided a view, then take a stab at describing the issue, using a "how can we . . . " phrase, balancing the main theme of the difference in the perspectives voiced. It might look like, "How can we improve/obtain/ensure X and Y?" The same principles noted on page 66 apply to a group. No matter how the issue is stated, the important things are:

- *Each person can see their perspective within it, room to talk about what they want to talk about.*
- *The language is non-judgmental, non-blaming, and balanced.*
- *It gives each participant the opportunity to address the heart of the matter, as they perceive it.*

Typically, a test for consensus about the issue statement can be a "thumbs up," an approval in principle.

Now the real work as a facilitator begins: helping people to identify the interests within their perspectives. It may seem as if you have to manage the interests of every participant within the group at once.

Remember that it is not the group that gives us trust as facilitators, it's each individual within it. As a facilitator, you can work with each individual, interpreting what you're hearing as their "want, or want to avoid." You will probably have made notes as each perspective was being voiced, and you probably have some idea from your own sense of the context about what interests people want to see reflected in a solution. Remember that you are capturing *their* interests. That requires their affirmation that you have done so accurately. If you didn't get it right, then try again.

Generating options from the interests is always that same question: "What could we do to resolve the issues we are working on in ways that would satisfy the interests we just noted?" I've already described the generation of options process that I use with groups, and the restrictions on examining, explaining, and justifying, any option proposed. This is essential. If this is not followed, early evaluation will kill all creativity in the room.

When the options have been generated, check to ensure that at least one option exists to reflect each interest identified. Then, as the facilitator you will ask them, "Is this idea a high, medium, or low?", while continuing to restrict any explanation for their rating. Alternatively, you can use the "high five" method that I mentioned, whereby you say to them:

> *We are going to do a quick poll to see how close we are to consensus on several of these options. It will be a show of fingers, not hands. Five fingers means you love the idea – wish it was yours. Four means you are very content with it. Three means you can live with it, even if you prefer a different idea. Two means you have serious concerns about this idea. One means you cannot live with it.*

When the options have been rated, you can do a mini-exchange about the ones where there are high and low discrepancies or where one or two fingers were raised, asking, "What is it that makes it a high/low for you?" Your last task, when discrepancies have been resolved, is to explore implementation and the next steps, testing with questions that start with how, who and when.

When I work with groups, I don't hesitate to lean on them to guide the process too. By that, I mean that process choices arise, and in the end it's their process, not mine. So, it's not uncommon for me to stop at a moment and think out loud about a couple of ways that we could proceed, and then look to the group for input. In my experience, that empowerment contributes to the process and helps to create group ownership of outcomes. If you think about it as analogous to the collective wisdom of a jury of twelve compared with that of a single judge, you will appreciate those judges who have expressed greater faith in that collective wisdom than in their own single opinion. I use a variety of tools to enhance group collaboration, and I'll share those in a follow-up publication because they deserve more attention and explanation than I can provide here.

To summarize on working within your group, when you are detached from a desired outcome, you can focus on process. The logic of the process works – trust it. While it's true that you are working with a group, at any moment you are mainly working one-on-one with a single participant in the presence of the group. Focus on the step you're on, and the individual with whom you're working. Many of the approaches used in a two-person conversation are applicable to groups with minimal adjustments to the phraseology above. The more comfortable the group becomes with the model, the more effective and unified your group will be.

Leading the Shift to Collaboration within Institutions

At the institutional level, we are talking about how to make a significant cultural change. While the magnitude of the challenge associated with this change may not match that of Galileo to shift institutions like the Catholic Church from thinking the universe was geocentric to accepting that it is heliocentric, it may not be so far off either. I certainly don't pretend to have the intellect of Galileo – I do empathize with his struggles though!

Where would we begin? *In Great Company*[47] notes it's almost impossible to change a culture if no change of language occurs. The first and absolutely fundamental change of language required is from conflict to tension. People don't experience the same angst around tension as they do around conflict – it seems less threatening. Everyone experiences tension in their relationships from their partners, to their parents, to their pets!

The second switch of language is the introduction of the concept of an adjudicative model to serve as a contrast with a collaborative one. Until people recognize that their patterns of communication, problem-solving, and analysis are based on an adjudicative model, they cannot conceive of another model, let alone one that is superior.

Those two significant shifts of language may be enough to trigger the change to collaboration, or at least to support it. As the shift from the language of conflict to the language of collaboration expands, systems change. For example, in the Canadian federal system, the role of a Mediator or Conflict Management Practitioner would be replaced with the title of Collaborative Process Facilitator. Language of workplace conflict would be replaced with workplace tension. Similarly, group processes, which are commonly called "interventions" in the field would be described as "workplace restorative processes." The current informal conflict management system would change title to informal collaborative support system. Language must change in order to inspire minds and hearts to change.

To achieve a change at the institutional level, we also need to employ principles of change management. If collaboration has both a task and a relationship element to it, then what would we use as a collaborative change management framework? From my analysis and study, no single change management model exists that really has both components. My proposal would be to use two approaches that are incredibly compatible, and which seem to anticipate the existence of the other, while retaining their primary focus. That is to say, I really

---

47 Quentin Jones, Corinne Canter, Dexter Dunphy, Rosalie Fishman, and Margherita Larné, *In Great Company: Unlocking the Secrets of Cultural Transformation* (Sydney, NSW: Human Synergistics International, 2011) Chapter 2.

like John Kotter's model[48] for leading change beginning with a strong vision in which the primary focus is on task.

I also really like William Bridges' model[49] for supporting people through the personal experience of change: transition, where the primary focus is on relationships. I would add that I think these go in this order: first change is led based on a vision, and then people are supported through their transition to achieve that vision. That said, I appreciate that those reading will say how I see change is not how they have experienced it!

Kotter states that there must be an urgent need for change, a burning platform. The concerns outlined above with the adjudicative model surely would indicate that the adjudicative model is a burning platform which will not support the pace or pressures of the modern era.

In order to create change, Kotter suggests that a vision of a desirable alternative is required. According to Kotter in *Leading Change*, a good vision statement has these characteristics (Kotter, 1996, 72):

1. Imaginable – Conveys a picture of what the future will look like

---

48 John P. Kotter, Leading Change (Boston: Harvard Business Review Press, 1996) 21. Kotter outlines his eight-step model: 1. Establish a sense of urgency. 2. Create a guiding coalition. 3. Develop a vision and strategy. 4. Communicate the change vision. 5. Empower broad-based action. 6. Generate short term wins. 7. Consolidate gains and make more change. 8. Anchor new approaches in the culture. As I read his description, I think that number three, the vision, is central to making the other steps work.

49 William Bridges, *Managing Transitions: Making the Most of Change* (Philadelphia: Perseus Books Group, 2009). Bridges describes the individual experience of change as transition that begins with what is ending. His model guides managers to support people through the ending, after which they enter a neutral zone, which is sort of disorganized chaos. In that Neutral zone, the old world no longer applies and the new one is not yet here, so people can influence how they want it to be (within limits.) Finally, the change process is implemented and the individual moves into new beginnings, where there is a new norm. Bridges' model, as I read it, is very focussed on the individual's experience and how to support that process. Bridges added check lists for supporting people through each phase – very useful.

2. Desirable – Appeals to the long-term interests of [stakeholders]
3. Feasible – Comprises realistic attainable goals
4. Focused – Is clear enough to provide guidance in decision-making
5. Flexible – Is general enough to allow individual initiative and alternative responses in light of changing conditions
6. Communicable – Is easy to communicate; can be successfully explained in five minutes

Taking those into consideration, my trial balloon of the vision of a culture of collaboration is this:

> The collaborative model would be widely used as the primary or default model for communication, problem-solving and analysis in society. In government, papers and briefing materials would be written in a sequence that mirrored the collaborative model. Basic training in the use of the model would be widespread. The model would be embedded in the same way that the adjudicative model is today. Leaders in all organizations, in both the private and public sectors, would have a collaborative orientation. Within organizations, starting with government, centers of expertise in collaboration and collaborative tools and processes would be developed to replace conflict management systems. The ability to facilitate a collaborative process and to use collaborative tools would be common, and at the same time, specialists or professionals would be available for more complex situations. The culture of collaboration would strengthen communication, relationships, and leadership in the community and at work, such that individuals, industry, and institutions would function at a higher level.

You will note that this book is not three hundred pages in length. It's about a hundred pages – even shorter than *Getting to Yes*. If it took me three hundred pages to explain why collaboration is simple, you should really doubt my premise!

If that's the vision, then who or what constitutes the "guiding coalition" about which Kotter speaks in step two of his change model? Room for leadership exists at all levels to move us toward this vision. At the upper level, the governmental organizations, the governing body in any nation, has a responsibility to lead advancement in society. Thinking primarily of the United States of America and Canada, whether nation and state, or federal and provincial, of course issues like shared or exclusive jurisdiction can arise. Those sorts of issues are about the authority to enact laws. That is not all or perhaps even primarily what change leadership is about. Policy adoption, endorsement, and support often have more impact than the enactment of a law.

In Canada, the ICMS network is in a position to provide leadership for a shift from a focus on conflict to a focus on collaboration. The ICMS is a joint labour and management initiative with representatives of government working in cooperation with representatives of collective bargaining. I'd like to think I've planted the seeds for that shift to collaboration in my having written the revised *ICMS Resource Guide*.

The third arena where I see an opportunity for influence is within the academic world. As Cardinal Newman suggested,[50] the idea of a university is not to get students a job; rather, it's to create the well-informed citizen, regardless of what employment (if any) they pursue. Today, most institutions of higher learning offer both training in the collaborative model and at the same time an abundance of courses where the problem-solving, analysis, and decision-making are based on the adjudicative model. This will be a waiting game to see who moves first!

In Canada, I could see institutions like the National Managers Community within the federal government playing a leadership role

---

50   John Henry Newman, *The Idea of a University Defined and Illustrated* ... 3rd ed. (London: Basil Montagu Pickering, 1873). Cardinal John Henry Newman suggested that the value of a liberal education is for the formation of citizens, not for obtaining employment.

in the development of a culture of collaboration. That entity has already developed a series of tools for leadership and learning which are very compatible with a culture of collaboration.

Whether in government, academic institutions, or private organizations and whether among groups or individuals, the strategies and tactics for implementation will vary to a great extent and will require effective change management and solid support.

Conclusion

The adjudicative model, which has served society since the days of early civilization, is no longer getting the job done as our world becomes increasingly diverse, inclusive, and complex. That model is deeply embedded, and a great deal of institutional culture has grown in alignment with it. That said, society has replaced many other models when they have ceased to be either acceptable or useful. Why can't we abandon the adjudicative model as the default and replace it?

The journey from ignorance to integration begins with awareness. Until we recognize that we are using an adjudicative model as the default, we cannot have a conversation about its weaknesses. Once aware of its weaknesses, then we can implement a significantly superior alternative model. This book has put a label on the default model, described its limitations, and has offered a generally superior model in order to start that conversation.

Now, it becomes a question of generating the collective will and momentum to progress to integration. Unfortunately, the seminal and important work *Getting to Yes* did not create the momentum needed. That's because the horse of collaboration was hitched to the wagon of conflict, and very few have wanted to take that ride. To continue the metaphor, our collaborative horse has been in its stall for almost four decades. It is time to unhitch collaboration from conflict and to unleash its power to deliver the dual outcomes of better solutions and stronger relationships in our workplaces.

The key is to use the collaborative model for communication. When the collaborative model is embedded in everyday communication, its use for more complex applications like analysis, decision- making, and problem-solving becomes a natural extension. As that progression continues, collaborative tools can become widely utilized, and society will progress towards integration of the collaborative model.

The journey from ignorance to integration is a challenging one for any advancement. I hope that I have adequately equipped you, as a reader, with information, explanations, and some tools to enable you to begin the journey within your workplace. Remember that while variations of collaborative approaches are taught extensively at many universities, they are also taught at elementary schools, and students use them on the playground. Using this new collaborative model is not rocket science, it's not brain surgery, and to mix metaphors, it's not even rocket surgery.

You may have noticed that your workplace is not interacting in an optimal way. Perhaps that is the reason why you are reading this book. Maybe you neither had a way to describe it before you read this book, nor a way to describe an alternative. Now, you do, and hopefully, this book provides you with easy ways to explain collaboration and this new collaborative model to colleagues who are not aware of its advantages. We know there is a huge gap in awareness around collaboration. We have no idea how much we do NOT know, no matter how much we do know. The gap is by definition impossible to quantify. By sharing the vision of a culture of collaboration, we narrow that gap, encourage others to adopt it, and support its implementation.

I hope you have enjoyed reading this book and will enjoy using this collaborative model in various roles and contexts. If you have questions, comments, or feedback, please email me at patrick@collaborativepath.ca. I would love to hear what you think.

Stay tuned for a companion to this book. I'm now turning my attention to assembling *The Collaborator's Toolbox*. These tools will help those who want to benefit from the use of the collaborative model within your homes, your workplaces, and your communities.

A Final Reflection

I struggled in writing this book with the question of where it fits in relation to *Getting to Yes*. As I noted early on, *Getting to Yes* is the foundational text for the whole field of Conflict Resolution. I also struggled with how my collaborative model intersects with Conflict Resolution. I have added this final reflection to elaborate upon my insights and thought process around these issues for what it's worth, and in case you're pondering those questions, too.

Getting to Yes introduced an innovative approach to negotiations where parties seemed fixed on positions. That is, some level of palpable tension could be expected at the point where its principled negotiations process would begin to be used. My collaborative model, if employed at that same point, honours the overarching framework of *Getting to Yes*. If employed from the outset, then there is a strong likelihood that the participants would reach an optimal solution and avoid that tension. My model represents an enhanced process with a greater level of detail about how to make it work before tension arises – in fact, it can be used as the default from the beginning of any interaction. Is my model better, easier to use, and more pragmatic than principled negotiations? Those are questions that only time and others can answer. I don't see it as a competition. It's my hope that in presenting my model, I have honoured the genius of *Getting to Yes*. It's my expectation that at some point, this book and its ideas will serve as a springboard for further innovation and refinement. Perhaps that's the way most innovative thinking works: it builds upon earlier thinking and ideas like I have done with *Getting to Yes*, not from a blank page. If my book serves as a springboard for others trying to make this world a better place, well, that will be incredibly satisfying. My vision is that this book becomes the impetus for widespread growth around collaboration, emanating from some centre of learning. Imagine the impact on the world that an initiative to be known as the "Collaboration Project" will have.

In relation to the whole field of Conflict Resolution, I did that work, performed the mediator role, and I know its power and value. That said, in order for the field to expand, I believe we have to change our language in order to escape the stigma associated with conflict. People generally are far more attracted to the idea of strengthening their capacity for collaboration than to resolving conflict. If changing language opens up a world of new opportunities and has no downside, then why *not* go there? Conflict Resolution clearly works. It's very cost effective. Yet, the issue is not about its value; the issue is about its lack of appeal to a broad base.

Finally, neither *Getting to Yes* nor the field of Conflict Resolution target the pre-conflict stage, only the active conflict period. Their target is the 20 percent, not the 80. A significant point of departure of this book from both *Getting to Yes* and the field of Conflict Resolution is that this book provides a means to address both the 80 and the 20 covered by the 80-20 rule. Again, the idea is to expand the scope of influence of both the framework of *Getting to Yes* and the practice of Conflict Resolution. Whereas both *Getting to Yes* and the field of Conflict Resolution address one situation at a time, thereby making this world a better place, this book has as its objective to create an entire culture of collaboration. Its targeted impact is global, encompassing all of society and creating a new default in order to impact the world in a positive way. In the end, *Getting to Yes*, the field of Conflict Resolution, and this book, have similar desired outcomes and the differences are in the lenses, tools, and processes to achieve those positive impacts.

I felt it was important to share my perspective on these issues as a final reflection, before I dive into the development of *The Collaborator's Toolbox* to further support the creation of a culture of collaboration.

About Patrick

Patrick describes himself as a "recovering lawyer." His career has included being a litigation lawyer, arbitrator, mediator, policy analyst, project manager and conflict management consultant. After an extensive private sector career, Patrick worked with several departments in the Canadian federal government. In addition, he has volunteered in many capacities.

Working in so many roles across sectors, Patrick has forged strong relationships and connected people and groups across spheres of involvement and platforms of change. His passion lies in the enhancement of relationships and problem-solving.

In his spare time, living by the ocean on Prince Edward Island, Patrick embraces a healthy, active lifestyle and has begun work on The Collaborator's Toolbox as a companion to this book.

Book Patrick Now

Hosting a conference? A group or divisional reorganization? Annual meeting?
What a wonderful opportunity to get things off to a great start!
Patrick can inspire your group to abandon an adjudicative approach and embrace a collaborative path to success. He will both inform and entertain – guaranteed no one will be bored. Visit www.collaborative-path.ca to see previews of Patrick in action, and listen to excerpts from his audio book.

Bulk Book Order Discount

Are you teaching a course or workshop and want to use this book as foundational learning for your curriculum and would need to order in volume?

Are you thinking that your enterprise, division or team would benefit tremendously if it were to adopt a collaborative approach?

Would you like to change how your group works – from an adjudicative model to a collaborative one?

Reach out to me at bookqueries@collaborativepath.ca, and let's see what we can do as a bulk discount to make your order of even ten or more cost effective!

Bibliography

Bercovitch, Jacob and Judith Fretter. *Regional Guide to International Conflict and Management from 1945 to 2003*. Washington, D.C.: CQ Press, 2004.

Bridges, William. *Managing Transitions: Making the Most of Change*. Philadelphia: Perseus Books Group, 2009.

Buckingham, Marcus and Curtis Coffman. *First, Break All the Rules: What the World's Greatest Managers Do Differently*. New York: Simon and Schuster, 1999.

Bush, Robert A. Baruch and Joseph Folger. *The Promise of Mediation: Responding to Conflict through Empowerment and Recognition*. San Francisco: Jossey-Bass, 1994.

Covey, Stephen R. *The 7 Habits of Highly Effective People: Restoring the Character Ethic*. New York: Free Press, 2004.

De Bono, Edward. *Six Thinking Hats: An Essential Approach to Business Management*. Boston: Little, Brown, 1985.

Fisher, Len. *The Perfect Swarm: The Science of Complexity in Everyday Life*. New York: Basic Books, 2009.

Fisher, Roger, and William Ury. *Getting to Yes: Negotiating Agreement Without Giving in*. New York: Penguin Books, 1981.

Fisher, Roger, William Ury and Bruce Patton. *Getting to Yes: Negotiating Agreement Without Giving In*, 2nd ed. New York: Penguin Press, 1991.

Fisher, Roger. *Beyond Reason: Using Emotions as You Negotiate.* New York: Penguin Books, 2006.

Gottman, John and Joan DeClaire. *The Relationship Cure: A 5 Step Guide to Strengthening Your Marriage, Family, and Friendships.* New York: Three Rivers Press, 2001.

Hall, Doug. *Jump Start Your Business Brain: Win More, Lose Less and Make More Money.* Cincinnati: Brain Brew Books, 2002.

Jones, Quentin, Corinne Canter, Dexter Dunphy, Rosalie Fishman, and Margherita Larné. *In Great Company: Unlocking the Secrets of Cultural Transformation.* Sydney, NSW: Human Synergistics International, 2011.

Kotter, John P. *Leading Change.* Boston: Harvard Business Review Press, 1996.

Kramer, Roderick M. *Negotiation as a Social Process.* Thousand Oaks, CA: Sage Publications, 1995.

Lencioni, Patrick. *The Five Dysfunctions of a Team.* San Francisco: Jossey-Bass, 2002.

Mehrabian, Albert. *Silent Messages: Implicit Communication of Emotions and Attitudes.* Belmont, CA: Wadsworth, 1972.

Newman, John Henry. *The Idea of a University Defined and Illustrated* ... , 3rd ed. London: Basil Montagu Pickering, 1873.

Redekop, Vern Neufeld. *From Violence to Blessing: How an Understanding of Deep-Rooted Conflict Can Open Paths to Reconciliation.* Ottawa: Novalis Publications, 2002.

Rosenberg, Marshall B. *Nonviolent Communication: A Language of Compassion.* San Diego, CA: Puddledancer Press, 2003.

Rundle, Craig E. *Becoming a Conflict Competent Leader: How You and Your Organization Can Manage Conflict Effectively.* San Francisco: Jossey-Bass, 2013.

Rundle, Craig E. and Tim A. Flanagan. *Building Conflict Competent Teams*. San Francisco: Jossey-Bass, 2008.

Stone, Douglas, Bruce Patton, and Sheila Heen. *Difficult Conversations: How to Discuss What Matters Most*. New York: Penguin Books, 1999.

Thomas, Kenneth W. and Ralph H. Kilmann. *Thomas-Kilmann Conflict Mode Instrument*. Tuxedo NY: Xicom, 1974.

Ury, William. *The Power of a Positive No: How to say No and Still Get to Yes*. New York: Bantam Books, 2007.

Printed in Canada